JONES & BARTLETT LEARNING INFORMATION SYSTEMS SECURITY & ASSURANCE SERIES

LABORATORY MANUAL TO ACCOMPANY

System Forensics, Investigation, and Response

VERSION 1.5

virtualsecurity CLOUD labs
powered by TOOLWIRE

VLAB SOLUTIONS

COMMITTEE ON NATIONAL SECURITY SYSTEMS
CNSS
SYSTEMS SECURITY FOR THE 21st CENTURY

The ISSA Series meets all of the elements of the Committee on National Security Systems (CNSS) National Training Standard for: *Information Systems Security (INFOSEC) Professionals, NSTISSI No. 4011 System Administrators, CNSSI No. 4013 Advanced Level*

JONES & BARTLETT LEARNING

World Headquarters
Jones & Bartlett Learning
5 Wall Street
Burlington, MA 01803
978-443-5000
info@jblearning.com
www.jblearning.com

Jones & Bartlett Learning books and products are available through most bookstores and online booksellers. To contact Jones & Bartlett Learning directly, call 800-832-0034, fax 978-443-8000, or visit our website, www.jblearning.com.

Substantial discounts on bulk quantities of Jones & Bartlett Learning publications are available to corporations, professional associations, and other qualified organizations. For details and specific discount information, contact the special sales department at Jones & Bartlett Learning via the above contact information or send an email to specialsales@jblearning.com.

Production Credits
Chief Executive Officer: Ty Field
President: James Homer
SVP, Editor-in-Chief: Michael Johnson
SVP, Curriculum Solutions: Christopher Will
Director of Sales, Curriculum Solutions: Randi Roger
Author: vLab Solutions, LLC, David Kim, President
Editorial Management: High Stakes Writing, LLC, Lawrence J. Goodrich, Editor and Publisher
Copy Editor, High Stakes Writing: Katherine Dillin
Copy Editor, High Stakes Writing: Ruth Walker
Senior Editorial Assistant: Rainna Erikson
Reprints and Special Projects Manager: Susan Schultz
Associate Production Editor: Tina Chen
Production Assistant: Kristin Rogers
Rights & Photo Research Associate: Lian Bruno
Manufacturing and Inventory Control Supervisor: Amy Bacus
Senior Marketing Manager: Andrea DeFronzo
Cover Design: Anne Spencer
Composition: CAE Solutions Corp.
Cover Image: © ErickN/ShutterStock, Inc.
Printing and Binding: Edwards Brothers Malloy
Cover Printing: Edwards Brothers Malloy

ISBN: 978-1-284-03753-1

6048
Printed in the United States of America
17 16 15 14 13   10 9 8 7 6 5 4 3 2 1

Contents

Ethics and Code of Conduct

The material presented in this course is designed to give you a real-life look at the use of various tools and systems that are at the heart of every network security analyst's daily responsibilities. Through use of this material, you will have access to software and techniques used every day by professionals. With this access come certain ethical responsibilities.

The hardware, software, tools, and applications presented and used in this lab manual and/or the VSCL are intended to be used for instructional and educational purposes only.

As a student in this course, you are not to use these tools, applications, or techniques on live production IT infrastructures inside or outside of your campus or organization. Under no circumstances are you permitted to use these tools, applications, or techniques on the production IT infrastructures and networks of other organizations.

You are required to conform to your school or organization's Code of Conduct and ethics policies during the use of this lab manual and any of the tools, applications, or techniques described within.

Preface

Welcome! This lab manual is your step-by-step guide to completing the laboratory exercises for this course.

Virtual Security Cloud Lab (VSCL)

For most of the exercises in this lab manual, you will use the Virtual Security Cloud Lab (VSCL) resource.

> **Note:**
> The Virtual Security Cloud Lab requires use of either **Windows Internet Explorer** or **Mozilla Firefox**. The Virtual Security Cloud Lab does not support Google Chrome, Safari, or Opera at this time.

The VSCL is a collection of virtual resources, including Windows and Linux servers, Cisco routers, and applications such as Wireshark, FileZilla, and Nessus®, that will allow you to perform all of the tasks in this lab manual as if you were performing them in a live production environment. The heart of the VSCL is a Windows Workstation desktop configured to give you access to the tools and resources you need for each lab, without any special setup on your part.

As noted in the following table, one of the exercises in this lab manual will be performed without using the VSCL. For detailed instructions on how to perform this exercise, please consult your syllabus or instructor.

How to Use This Lab Manual

This lab manual features step-by-step instructions for completing the following hands-on lab exercises:

VSCL	LAB TITLE
Yes	Lab #1: Perform a Byte-Level Computer Audit
No	Lab #2: Apply the Daubert Standard on the Workstation Domain
Yes	Lab #3: Create a Forensic System Case File for Analyzing Forensic Evidence
Yes	Lab #4: Uncover New Digital Evidence Using Bootable Utilities
Yes	Lab #5: Automate Digital Evidence Discovery Using Paraben's P2 Commander
Yes	Lab #6: Apply Steganography to Uncover Modifications to an Image File
Yes	Lab #7: Decode an FTP Protocol Session and Perform Forensic Analysis
Yes	Lab #8: Automate Image Evaluations and Identify Suspicious or Modified Files
Yes	Lab #9: Craft an Evidentiary Report for a Digital Forensic Case
Yes	Lab #10: Perform an Incident Response Investigation for a Suspicious Logon

Video Walkthroughs of Each Lab

Each VSCL-based exercise in this lab manual includes a video walkthrough that gives you a quick overview of every step and function. You can watch the video walkthrough prior to performing the lab exercise, and refer to it as necessary while you complete the lab. You can pause, rewind, and fast-forward the video walkthroughs if you need to take notes or spend extra time on a particular step or function. Consult your syllabus or instructor for information on where to locate the walkthrough videos.

Step-by-Step Instructions

You'll find it easy to complete these lab exercises by following the detailed step-by-step instructions. Each step is clearly broken down into sub-steps, and all actions you are required to take are noted in **bold** font. Screenshots are included to help you identify key menus, dialog boxes, and input locations. If you get stuck on a step, refer to the lab video, which follows the order of the steps.

Deliverables

At the completion of each lab, you'll be asked to provide a set of deliverables to your instructor. These deliverables may include documents, files, screenshots, and/or answers to assessment questions. The deliverables are designed to test your understanding of the information, and your successful completion of the steps and functions of the lab. For specific information on deliverables, refer to the **Deliverables** section at the end of each lab.

> **Note:**
> Some labs require the use of a word processor such as Microsoft® Word for preparing and submitting deliverables. If you do not have access to a word processor, you can use OpenOffice on the Workstation desktop of the VSCL to prepare your documents. It includes a word processor called Writer that has all the features necessary for creating documents for use in these labs.

File Transfer

At times, you may be asked to transfer to another computer files you have created while performing lab steps in the VSCL. This can be performed using the File Transfer function built in to the vWorkstation desktop of the VSCL. Instructions for preparing and sending files using the File Transfer function can be found at the beginning of the video walkthrough for the first lab in each course (in most cases, Lab #1).

> **Note:**
> Use of this lab manual or the VSCL **does not require use of the textbook.** If you have questions about whether a textbook is needed for your course, consult your instructor.

Perform a Byte-Level Computer Audit

LAB 1

Introduction

In this lab, you will use the Virtual Security Cloud Lab (VSCL) to perform a forensic analysis using the WinAudit, DevManView, and WinHex tools. You will review the different forensic capabilities of each tool, using the sample files provided, to determine any clandestine threats and vulnerabilities such as viruses and malicious software, if any. It should be noted that use of these tools alters data on the machine under investigation, potentially violating the chain of custody if performed on the original source system without write-blocking technologies in place. Screen captures of the drive or device in question should be created in order for external forensic analysis.

Learning Objectives

Upon completing this lab, you will be able to:

- Use WinAudit to identify computer system and software configuration details
- Use DevManView to identify system devices and configuration details
- Use WinHex to perform a byte-level file examination
- Identify correct file type for a misnamed file and inspect file contents following correction
- Create a report that contains details discovered during the computer audit

TOOLS AND SOFTWARE	
NAME	MORE INFORMATION
DevManView	http://www.nirsoft.net/utils/device_manager_view.html
WinAudit	http://www.pxserver.com/WinAudit.htm
WinHex	http://www.x-ways.net/winhex/

Deliverables

Upon completion of this lab, you are required to provide the following deliverables to your instructor:

1. A text document containing screen captures of the following:
   a. Computer audit details discovered using the WinAudit utility;
   b. System details discovered using the DevManView utility;
   c. Selected file type and file content description for target.abc;
2. Lab Assessment Questions & Answers for Lab #1.

Hands-On Steps

1. This lab begins at the student landing vWorkstation virtual machine desktop of the VSCL, as shown here.

FIGURE 1.1

"Student Landing" VSCL workstation

> **Note:**
> The next steps will use WinAudit to explore the configuration of the vWorkstation computer. You will record the information you uncover as a deliverable for this lab.

2. **Double-click** the **My Computer icon** on the desktop.
3. **Double-click** the **Local Disk (C:) icon**.
4. **Double-click** the **Forensic_Tools folder** to explore the tool options available.
5. **Double-click** the **winaudit folder**.
6. **Double-click** the **winaudit.exe file** to start the application.
7. **Click** the word **Here** in the center of the page to begin the audit process.

   The audit scans your computer and returns comprehensive information about the software and utilities it uncovers.

FIGURE 1.2

The WinAudit welcome screen

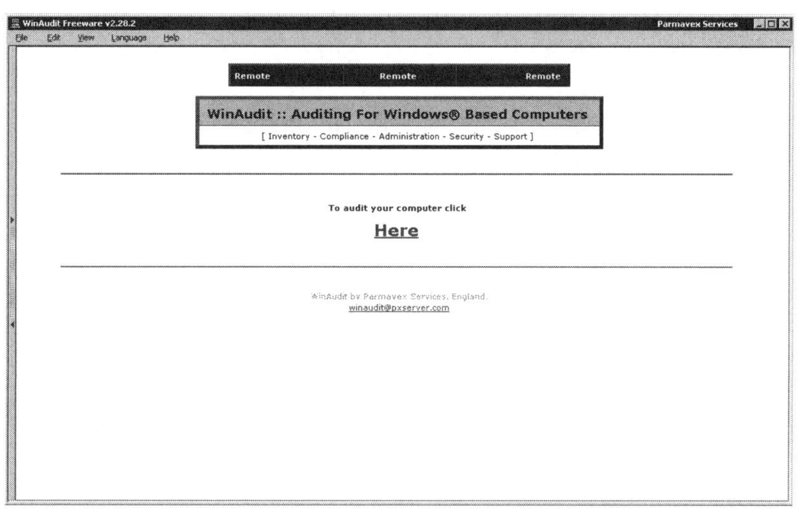

8. **Click** the **System Overview icon** in the left pane of the window.

   The System Overview page includes details about your computer such as the computer name, domain name, serial number, and system memory.

FIGURE 1.3

The System Overview audit

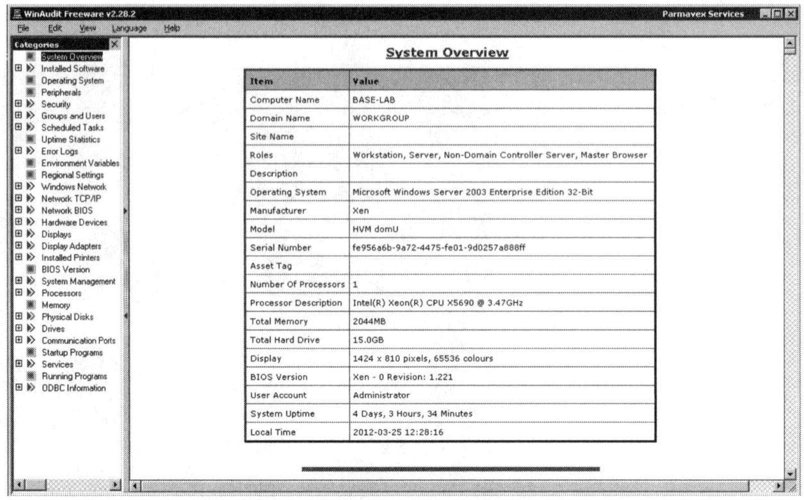

9. **Make a screen capture** of the System Overview findings and **paste** it into a new text document.

> **Note:**
>
> To capture the screen, **press** the **Ctrl** and **PrtSc** keys together, and then **use Ctrl + V** to paste the image into a Word or other word processor document.

10. **Click** the **Security icon** in the left pane of the WinAudit window to expand that category.
11. **Click** the **Windows Firewall icon** in the left pane.

    This page displays information about firewall settings, including information about authorized services and users.
12. **Make a screen capture** of the Windows Firewall findings and **paste** it into the text document.
13. **Click** the **Groups and Users icon** to expand that category.
14. **Click** the **User Accounts icon** to see specific information about the authorized user accounts for this computer.
15. **Make a screen capture** of the User Accounts findings and **paste** it into the text document.
16. **Click** the **Drives icon** in the left pane to gather information about the space available on each drive and the percentage used.
17. **Click** the **Drive C icon** to see specific information about that drive.
18. **Make a screen capture** of the Drive C findings and **paste** it into the text document.
19. Use the **File Transfer button** to download the **text file** to your local computer and submit it as part of your deliverables.
20. **Close** the **WinAudit window**. **Click No** if prompted to save the report before exiting.
21. **Close** the **C:\Forensic_Tools\winaudit folder** on the desktop.

Note:

The next steps will use the DevManView (Device Manager View) tool, similar to Windows Device Manager, to identify system devices and configuration details. You will record the information you uncover as a deliverable for this lab.

22. **Double-click** the **My Computer icon** on the desktop.
23. **Double-click** the **Local Disk (C:) icon**.
24. **Double-click** the **Forensic_Tools folder** to explore the tool options available.
25. **Double-click** the **devmanview folder**.
26. **Double-click** the **devmanview.exe file** to start the application.
27. **Click** the **Device Type Name column header** to sort the sheet by device type.

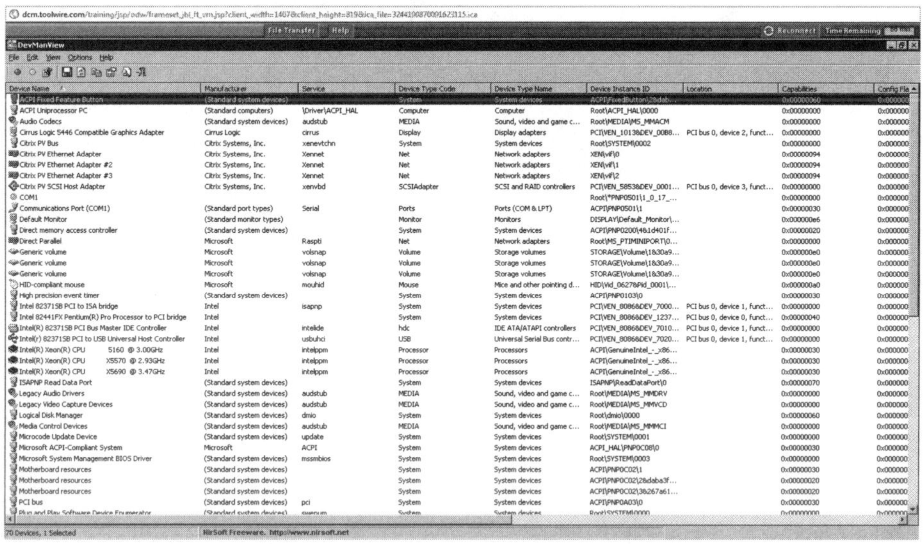

FIGURE 1.4
The DevManView window

28. **Click** the **DVD/CD-ROM drives** line item.
29. **Click** the **Device Name column header** to sort the sheet by device name.
30. **Scroll** down the list, **hold** the **CTRL key**, and **click** the **System CMOS/real time clock** line item to select it.
31. With both line items visible, **make a screen capture** of the DevManView sheet and **paste** it into a new text document.

Note:

To capture the screen, **press** the **Ctrl** and **PrtSc** keys together, and then **use Ctrl + V** to paste the image into a Word or other word processor document.

32. Use the **File Transfer button** to download the **text file** to your local computer and submit it as part of your deliverables.
33. **Close** the **DevManView window**.

> **Note:**
> The next steps will use the WinHex tool to perform an analysis of an unknown file type to make sure it is not malicious. You will record the information you uncover as a deliverable for this lab.

34. **Click** the **Back button** in the Forensic_Tools folder on the desktop.
35. **Double-click** the **winhex folder.**
36. **Double-click** the **winhex.exe file** to start the application.
37. If necessary, **resize** the **WinHex window** so that it is fully visible.

FIGURE 1.5
The WinHex window

38. **Click File** > **Open** from the WinHex toolbar.
39. In the Open Files dialog box, **navigate** to the **C:\Security_Strategies\SystemForensics folder**.
40. **Double-click** the **target.abc file** to open it in WinHex.

FIGURE 1.6
The Open Files dialog box in WinHex

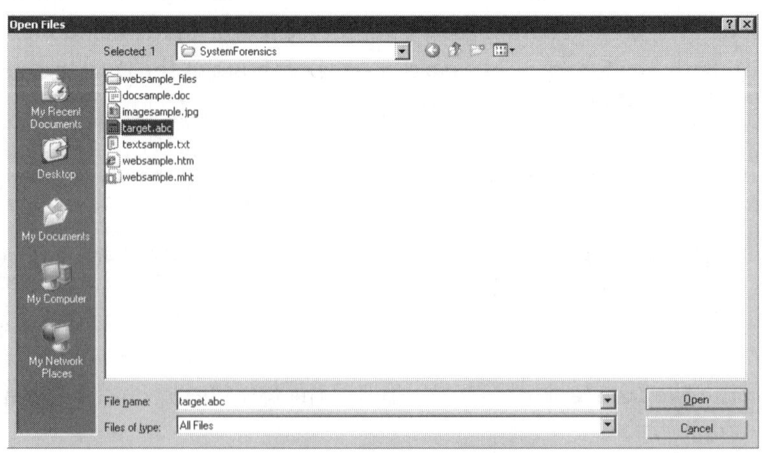

The file opens with the byte-level data of the file itself. The JFIF (an abbreviation for JPEG file interchange format) provides a good clue to the possible file type. It is most likely an image file.

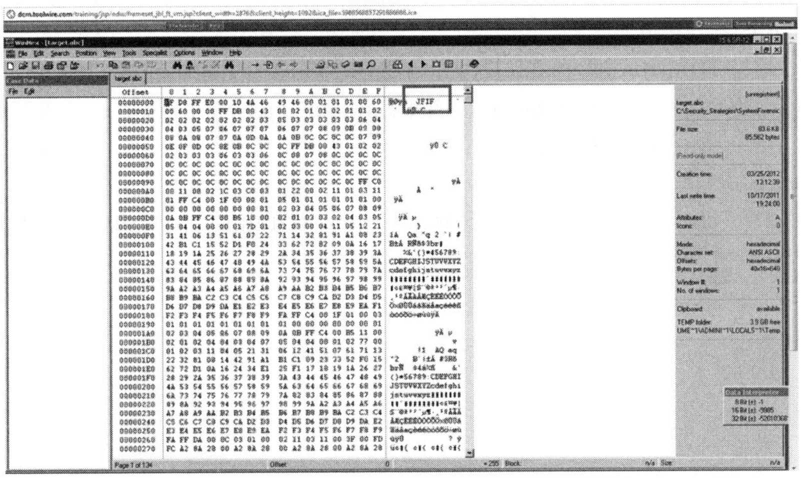

FIGURE 1.7
The byte-level data of the target.abc file indicating a clue

41. **Make a screen capture** of the WinHex window and **paste** it into a new text document.

> **Note:**
> To capture the screen, **press** the **Ctrl** and **PrtSc** keys together, and then **use Ctrl + V** to paste the image into a Word or other word processor document.

42. **Close** the **WinHex window.**
43. **Click** the **Back button twice** in the Forensic_Tools folder on the desktop.
44. **Double-click** the **Security_Strategies folder.**
45. **Double-click** the **SystemForensics folder.**
46. **Right-click** the **target.abc file** and **select Rename** from the context menu.
47. **Type target.jpg** to rename the file.
48. **Double-click** the **target.jpg file** to open it and make note of what you find.
49. **Make a screen capture** of the target.jpg image and **paste** it into the text document.
50. Use the **File Transfer button** to download the **text file** to your local computer and submit it as part of your deliverables.
51. **Close** the **target.jpg file.**
52. **Close** the **SystemForensics folder.**

Evaluation Criteria and Rubrics

The following are the evaluation criteria and rubrics for Lab #1 that the students must perform:

1. Was the student able to use WinAudit to identify computer system and software configuration details? – [**20%**]
2. Was the student able to use DevManView to identify system devices and configuration details? – [**20%**]
3. Was the student able to use WinHex to perform a byte-level file examination? – [**20%**]
4. Was the student able to identify correct file type for a misnamed file and inspect file contents following correction? – [**20%**]
5. Was the student able to create a report that contains details discovered during the computer audit? – [**20%**]

LAB #1 – ASSESSMENT WORKSHEET

Perform a Byte-Level Computer Audit

Course Name and Number: ____________________

Student Name: ____________________

Instructor Name: ____________________

Lab Due Date: ____________________

Overview

In this lab, you used the Virtual Security Cloud Lab (VSCL) to perform a forensic analysis using the WinAudit, DevManView, and WinHex tools. You reviewed the different forensic capabilities of each tool, using the sample files provided, to determine any clandestine threats and vulnerabilities such as viruses and malicious software, if any. It should be noted that use of these tools alters data on the machine under investigation, potentially violating the chain of custody if performed on the original source system without write-blocking technologies in place. Screen captures of the drive or device in question should be created in order for external forensic analysis.

Lab Assessment Questions & Answers

1. What is the main purpose of a software tool like WinAudit in computer forensics?

____

____

____

____

2. Which item(s) within WinAudit's System Overview report would you consider to be of critical importance in a computer forensic investigation?

____

____

____

____

3. Could you run WinAudit from a flash drive or any other external media? If so, why is this important during a computer forensic investigation?

4. Why would you use a tool like DevManView while performing a computer forensic investigation?

5. Which item(s) within DevManView's report would you consider to be of critical importance in a computer forensic investigation?

6. What tool similar to DevManView is already present in Microsoft® Windows systems?

7. Why would someone use a Hex editor during a forensic investigation?

8. What "clue" in your examination of WinHex leads you to the proper extension for the target.abc file?

9. What was the proper extension of the file you analyzed using WinHex? How did you find it?

10. Why do you need to keep evidence untampered with?

LAB 2

Apply the Daubert Standard on the Workstation Domain

Introduction

In this lab, you will conduct several Internet searches to investigate the major topics covered by the Daubert Standard and how they have been applied to court cases involving digital evidence and expert testimony. You will document the results of that research and apply the knowledge gained from it in another report based on the scenario described in this lab.

This lab is a paper-based design lab and does not require use of the Virtual Security Cloud Lab (VSCL). To successfully complete the deliverables for this lab, you will need access to a text editor or word processor, such as Microsoft® Word. For some labs, you may also need access to a graphics line drawing application, such as Visio or PowerPoint.

> **Note:**
> If you don't have a word processor or graphics package, use OpenOffice on the student landing vWorkstation for your lab deliverables and to answer the lab assessment questions. To capture screenshots, **press Prt Sc > MSPAINT**, **paste** into a text document, and **save** the document in the Security_Strategies folder (**C:\Security_Strategies**) using the File Transfer function.

Learning Objectives and Outcomes

Upon completing this lab, you will be able to:

- Analyze the legal admissibility of evidence based on the basic concepts used by the Daubert Standard
- Distinguish between a question of law and a question of fact
- Identify the differences between personal knowledge, hearsay, and opinion to analyze the type of testimony offered by an expert
- Recognize the difference between lay testimony and expert testimony
- List the general workflow steps that are dictated by the Daubert Standard when evaluating any theory as expert testimony (this includes scientific methodology, peer review and publication, the reliability of statistical information, and the theory's general acceptance by the scientific community)

Deliverables

Upon completion of this lab, you are required to provide the following deliverables to your instructor:

1. Daubert Standard Research Report;
2. Neo Case Study Lab #2;
3. Lab Assessment Questions & Answers for Lab #2.

Hands-On Steps

1. This lab begins at a workstation with Internet access. **Double-click** any **Internet browser icon** on your desktop to open the application.

> **Note:**
> The next steps will guide you through the steps you will take to complete the Daubert Standard Research Report.

2. In a new text document, **create** a **Daubert Standard Research Report.**

   You will follow the steps in this lab to complete a research report. You will be responsible for determining what to document in this report.
3. In your browser's address box, **type http://caselaw.lp.findlaw.com/scripts/getcase.pl?court=us&vol=509&invol=579** to review the U.S. Supreme Court case, Daubert v. Merrell Dow Pharmaceuticals, Inc.
4. In your browser's address box, **type google.com** to open the search tool.
5. From the Google search page, **research** the following items:
   - Federal Rules of Evidence, Article VII
   - What is the Frye Standard and where is it still admissible
   - Which justices dissented in the Daubert case
   - How does the Daubert Standard influence international law
   - Differences between law and fact (and judicial discretion)
   - Differences among personal knowledge, hearsay, and opinion
   - Differences between lay testimony and expert testimony
   - What skills are required by an expert witness
   - General workflow steps dictated by the Daubert Standard when evaluating any theory as expert testimony, including scientific methodology:
     - Whether the theories and techniques employed by the scientific expert have been tested
     - Whether they have been subjected to peer review and publication
     - Whether the techniques employed by the expert have a known error rate
     - Whether they are subject to standards governing their application
     - The reliability of statistical information
     - Whether the theories and techniques employed by the expert enjoy widespread (general) acceptance
6. In your text document, **record** a summary of the Daubert case and a summary of your findings from your research in step 5.
7. **Submit** the **text document** to your instructor as a deliverable for this lab.

> **Note:**
> The next steps will guide you through the steps you will take to complete the Neo Case Study Lab #2.

8. **Review** the following Neo Case Study:

   Neo is a hacker who was caught hacking into a Dallas-based company and stealing credit card information. Forensic evidence was obtained, and the zipped file with the credit cards on the victim's computer matched the zipped file on Neo's computer. The local police force brought you in to conduct the forensic investigation. You have a number of information security certifications, including CISSP®, and have been a practitioner for more than 10 years but do not have a private investigator's license in Texas. The defense is arguing that you are not qualified to present forensic evidence because of the lack of a PI license, per Texas state law. The prosecution is arguing that a PI license should not be required to conduct computer investigations because of your expert knowledge and your experience in forensics.

9. In a new text document, **create** a **Neo Case Study Lab** #2.

   You will follow the steps in this lab to complete this case study report. You will be responsible for determining what to document in this report.

10. In your text document, use your knowledge of the Daubert Standard, the Federal Rules of Evidence, Google research, and PI licensing in computer forensics to **draft** an argument stating why a PI license should or should not be required to conduct the investigation. If your conclusion is that a PI license should be required, then include your arguments to the prosecution stating why they should find another investigator who already has a PI license to perform the investigation for this case.

11. **Submit** the **text document** to your instructor as a deliverable for this lab.

Evaluation Criteria and Rubrics

The following are the evaluation criteria and rubrics for Lab #2 that the students must perform:

1. Was the student able to analyze the legal admissibility of evidence based on the basic concepts used by the Daubert Standard? – [**20%**]
2. Was the student able to distinguish between a question of law and a question of fact? – [**20%**]
3. Was the student able to identify the differences between personal knowledge, hearsay, and opinion to analyze the type of testimony offered by an expert? – [**20%**]
4. Was the student able to recognize the difference between lay testimony and expert testimony? – [**20%**]
5. Was the student able to list the general workflow steps that are dictated by the Daubert Standard when evaluating any theory as expert testimony? – [**20%**]

LAB #2 – ASSESSMENT WORKSHEET

Apply the Daubert Standard on the Workstation Domain

Course Name and Number: _______________

Student Name: _______________

Instructor Name: _______________

Lab Due Date: _______________

Overview

In this lab, you conducted several Internet searches to investigate the major topics covered by the Daubert Standard and how they have been applied to court cases involving digital evidence and expert testimony. You documented the results of that research and applied the knowledge gained from it in another report based on the scenario described in this lab.

Lab Assessment Questions & Answers

1. What is the presumption of innocence?

2. What is hearsay? Provide an example of when computer evidence can be considered hearsay.

3. What is system integrity?

4. Based on your research, could anybody be used as an expert witness?

5. What skills are required by an expert witness?

6. Do these expert witness requirements apply nationwide? Explain.

7. What is the definition of "scientific knowledge" under the Daubert Standard?

8. Give a brief summary of the Daubert v. Merrell Dow Pharmaceuticals case that you read.

9. What was the outcome of the case?

10. What previous Supreme Court ruling was superseded by the Federal Rules of Evidence as the standard for admitting expert scientific testimony?

11. Where is the Frye standard still admissible?

12. Where does Daubert put the responsibility of the admissibility of evidence?

13. What other cases are related to Daubert?

14. What is the influence of the Daubert Standard internationally?

15. Which justices dissented in Daubert?

Create a Forensic System Case File for Analyzing Forensic Evidence

LAB 3

Introduction

Any time forensic investigators explore a machine in search of evidence, they risk changing the very data they seek, potentially invalidating evidence. For this reason, they make use of tools, like Paraben's P2 Commander, that incorporate write-blocking technologies. The VSCL uses an image of an evidence drive to perform an investigation. In this lab, you will use P2 Commander to create an electronic case file showing the creation of a case and the addition of the evidence file provided to you, and you will save the case for review later. In this way, you will experience all of the steps necessary for the beginning of a sound forensic investigation.

Learning Objectives

Upon completing this lab, you will be able to:

- Create a new digital forensic case file using Paraben's P2 Commander forensics application
- Document a new digital forensic case with digital evidence submitted to the newly created case file
- Add a forensic system image evidence to the case file
- Save the digital forensic case file for further review
- Explain how to properly document and create a digital forensic case file as per the chain of custody

TOOLS AND SOFTWARE

NAME	MORE INFORMATION
P2 Commander	http://www.paraben.com/p2-commander.html

Deliverables

Upon completion of this lab, you are required to provide the following deliverables to your instructor:

1. Text document that includes a screen capture of the digital forensics case file and chain-of-custody date/timestamp documentation of your actions taken during this lab;
2. Lab Assessment Questions & Answers for Lab #3.

Hands-On Steps

1. This lab begins at the student landing vWorkstation virtual machine desktop of the VSCL, as shown here.

FIGURE 3.1

"Student Landing" VSCL workstation

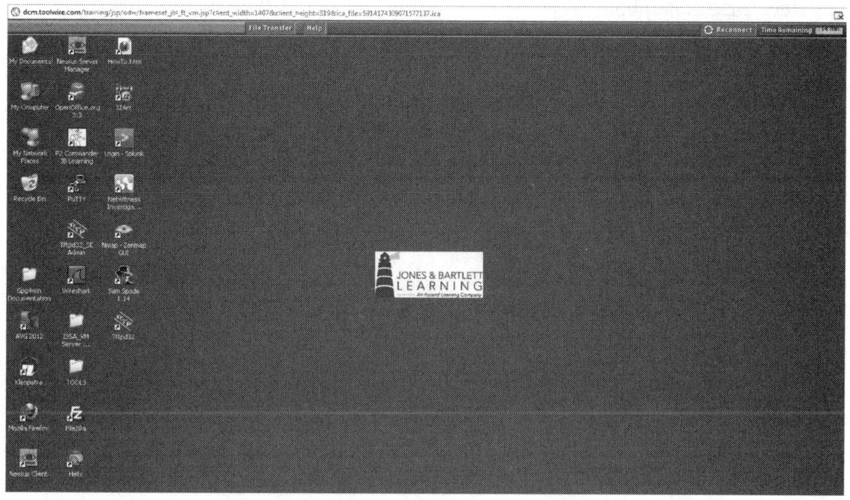

> **Note:**
> The next steps will use Paraben's P2 Commander to create a new forensic case file, add image evidence from the lab, and save the file for later use. You will document this process as a deliverable for this lab.

2. **Double-click** the **P2 Commander JB Learning icon** on the desktop to open the application.

   The P2 Commander's welcome screen opens with a navigation box entitled *Start your work here* at the left containing links to the most common activities that forensic investigators will perform within the tool.

3. **Click** the **Create new case link** in the left navigation box.

FIGURE 3.2

The P2 Commander welcome screen

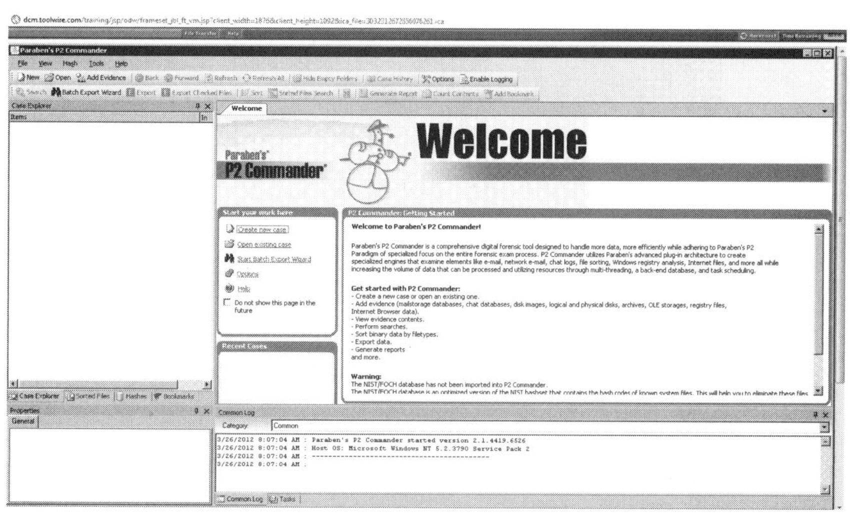

4. In the New Case dialog box, **click** the **Case Properties tab**.
5. **Type Lab #3 Digital Forensic Case File** in the Case name box.

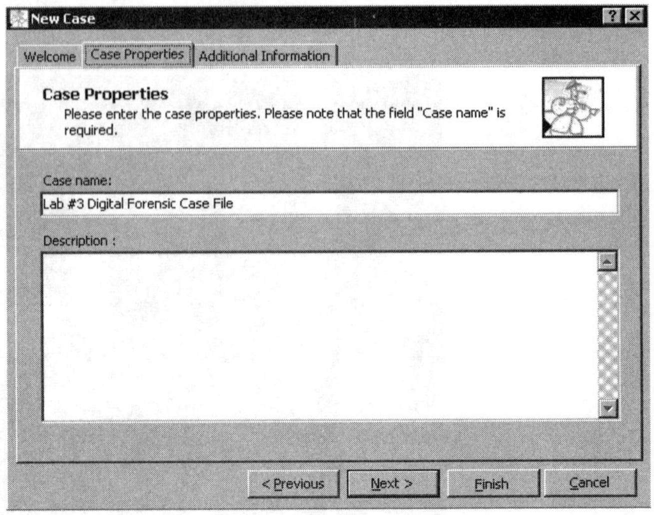

FIGURE 3.3
The New Case dialog box

6. **Click** the **Additional Information tab** to continue.
7. **Type *your name*** in the Investigator's name box and **click** the **Finish button**.
8. In the New case creation dialog box, **type Lab #3 Digital Forensic Case File** in the File name box, if necessary.
9. **Click Save** to create the new case file.

   A Lab #3 Digital Forensic Case File tab is added to the P2 Commander screen and the Add New Evidence dialog box opens.

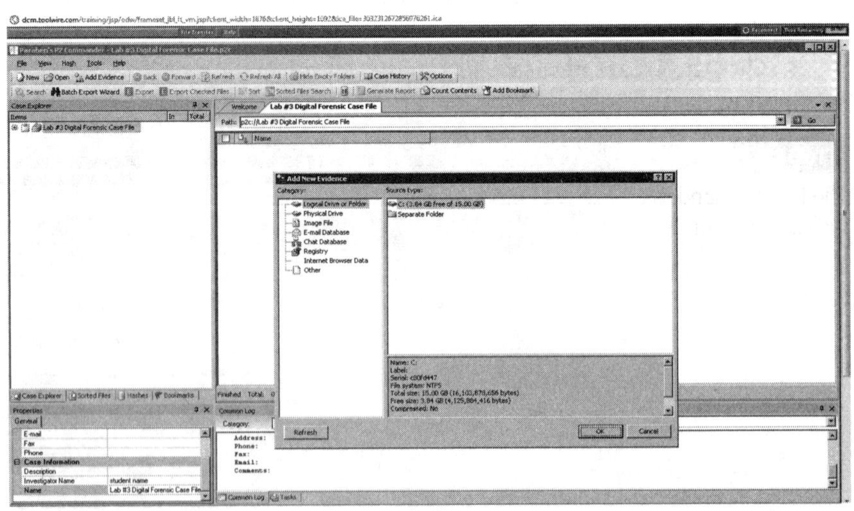

FIGURE 3.4
The Add New Evidence dialog box

10. **Click Image File** in the left pane of the Add New Evidence dialog box.
11. **Click Drive image** in the right pane and **click OK**.

FIGURE 3.5

Adding evidence to the case file

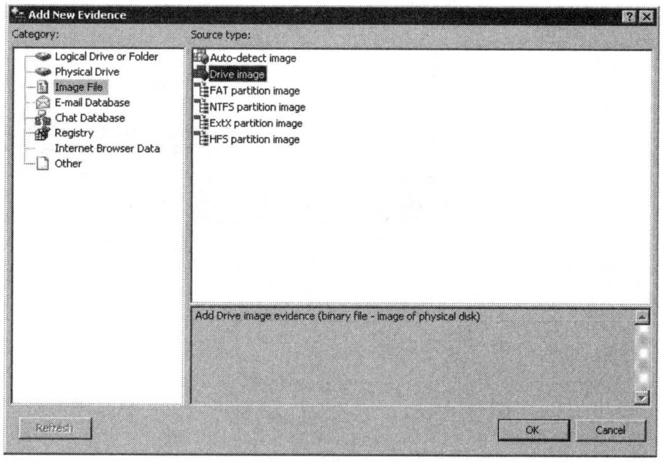

12. In the Open dialog box, **navigate** to the **C:\Forensic_Tools\vm_image folder**, **select** the **evidence_drive.e01.E01 file**, and **click Open**.
13. In the Enter a new evidence name box, **type Lab #3 Forensic Analysis** and **click OK** to add the data from this file to your case file.

FIGURE 3.6

Identifying the digital image file

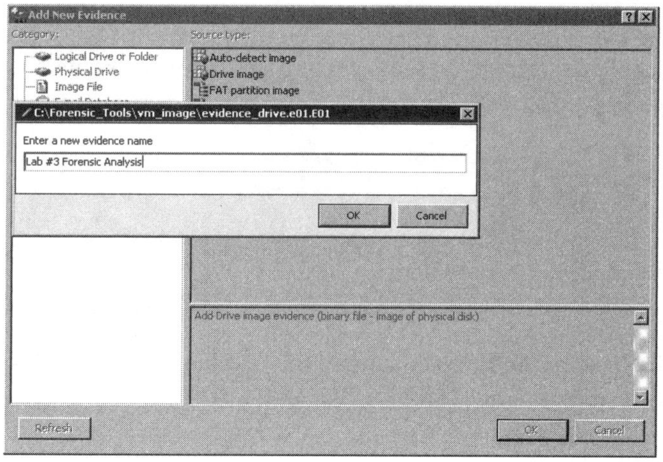

14. **Double-click Lab #3 Forensic Analysis** in the right pane of the P2 Commander.
15. **Double-click Partition Parser**.
16. **Double-click Partition0**.

    The NTFS dialog box will pop up.

FIGURE 3.7

NTFS Settings dialog box

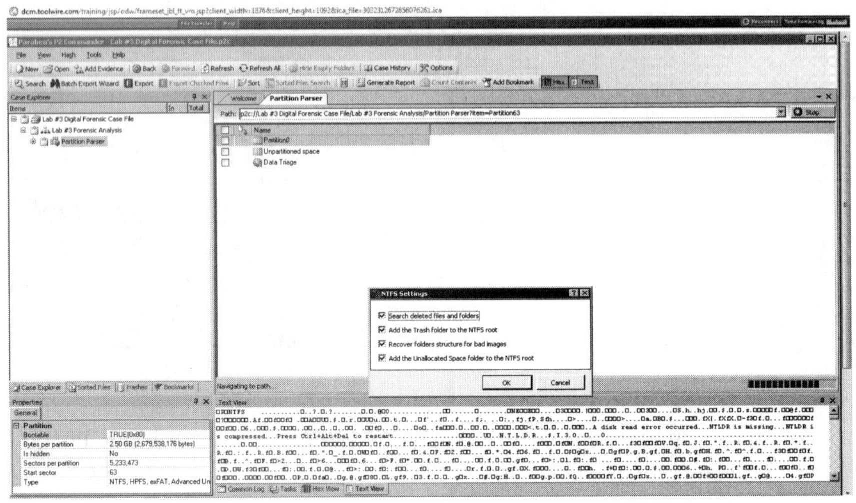

17. **Verify** that all options in the NTFS Settings dialog box are checked and **click OK**.
18. **Double-click NTFS** in the right pane.
19. **Double-click** the **Root folder** to see the file structure of the evidence image.
20. **Make a screen capture** of the P2 Commander window and **paste** it into a new text document.

> **Note:**
>
> To capture the screen, **press** the **Ctrl** and **PrtSc** keys together, and then **use Ctrl + V to paste the image into a** Word or other word processor document.

21. Use the **File Transfer button** to download the **text file** to your local computer and submit it as part of your deliverables.
22. **Click File > Save As** in the toolbar.

23. In the Save As dialog box, **type Lab #3 Digital Forensic Case File** in the File name box and **click Save**.

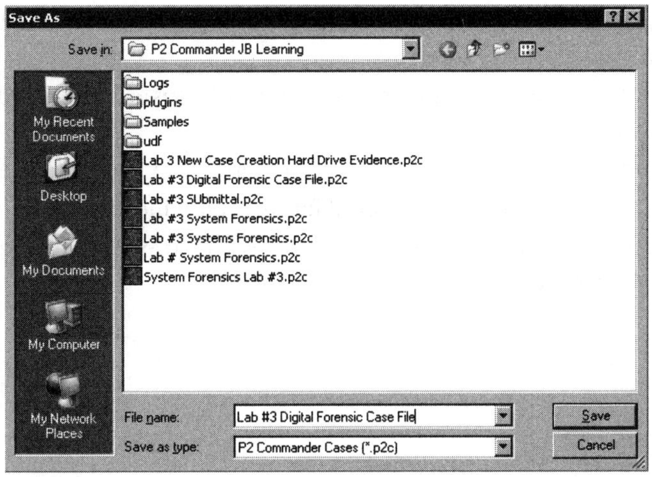

FIGURE 3.8

Saving the digital case file

24. **Click Yes** to confirm your wish to overwrite the existing case file that you created at the beginning of this lab.
25. Use the **File Transfer button** to download the **Lab #3 Digital Forensic Case File** to your local computer and submit it as part of your deliverables.
26. **Close** the **P2 Commander window**.

Evaluation Criteria and Rubrics

The following are the evaluation criteria and rubrics for Lab #3 that the students must perform:

1. Was the student able to create a new digital forensic case file using Paraben's P2 Commander forensic application? – **[20%]**
2. Was the student able to document a new digital forensic case with digital evidence submitted to the newly created case file? – **[20%]**
3. Was the student able to add a forensic system image evidence to the case file? – **[20%]**
4. Was the student able to save the digital forensic case file for further review? – **[20%]**
5. Was the student able to explain how to properly document and create a digital forensic case file as per the chain of custody? – **[20%]**

LAB #3 – ASSESSMENT WORKSHEET

Create a Forensic System Case File for Analyzing Forensic Evidence

Course Name and Number: ____________________

Student Name: ____________________

Instructor Name: ____________________

Lab Due Date: ____________________

Overview

Any time forensic investigators explore a machine in search of evidence, they risk changing the very data they seek, potentially invalidating evidence. For this reason, they make use of tools, like Paraben's P2 Commander, that incorporate write-blocking technologies. The VSCL uses an image of an evidence drive to perform an investigation. In this lab, you used P2 Commander to create an electronic case file showing the creation of a case and the addition of the evidence file provided to you, and you saved the case for review later. In this way, you experienced all of the steps necessary for the beginning of a sound forensic investigation.

Lab Assessment Questions & Answers

1. What is the main purpose of a forensic analysis?

____

____

____

____

2. What is the purpose of Paraben's P2 Commander?

____

____

____

____

3. Describe how the P2 Commander helps protect the chain of custody process.

4. Explain why it is a good idea to make an image or copy of the targeted image when conducting a forensic case analysis.

5. Describe in your own words why it is so important to properly document and create cases to house all the relevant forensic information pertaining to an investigation.

Uncover New Digital Evidence Using Bootable Utilities

LAB 4

Introduction

Any time forensic investigators explore a machine in search of evidence, they risk changing the very data they seek, potentially invalidating evidence. For this reason, they make use of tools that incorporate write-blocking technologies. The VSCL uses an image of an evidence drive to perform an investigation. In this lab, you will load various forensic applications and tools and run them locally on the target workstation or server under investigation. You will become familiar with the features and functions of the forensic applications in this lab: FavoritesView, IECacheView, IECookiesView, IEHistoryView, Helix, MyLastSearch, and Process Explorer.

Learning Objectives

Upon completing this lab, you will be able to:

- Load and run the Helix bootable utilities application
- Use the Helix utilities to identify system state and potential evidence in a forensically sound manner while working with a running system
- Apply a variety of utilities to identify data of potential evidentiary value while sustaining the state of the system and preserving forensic integrity
- Identify which forensic evidence or investigation tool can be used to conduct various forensic investigations that can be submitted as evidence in a court of law
- Create a report presenting details of running processes and browser usage for the landing vWorkstation

TOOLS AND SOFTWARE

NAME	MORE INFORMATION
FavoritesView	http://www.nirsoft.net/utils/faview.html
Helix	http://www.e-fense.com/products.php
IECacheView	http://www.nirsoft.net/utils/ie_cache_viewer.html
IECookiesView	http://www.nirsoft.net/utils/iecookies.html
IEHistoryView	http://www.nirsoft.net/utils/iehv.html
MyLastSearch	http://www.nirsoft.net/utils/my_last_search.html
Process Explorer	http://technet.microsoft.com/en-us/sysinternals/bb896653

Deliverables

Upon completion of this lab, you are required to provide the following deliverables to your instructor:

1. Text document that includes screen captures of your findings from each of the forensic analysis tools you explored in this lab;
2. Lab Assessment Questions & Answers for Lab #4.

Hands-On Steps

1. This lab begins at the student landing vWorkstation virtual machine desktop of the VSCL, as shown here.

FIGURE 4.1

"Student Landing" VSCL workstation

Note:

The next steps will use the Helix tool to find a series of specific data items. You will document these items in a text document as a deliverable for this lab.

2. **Double-click** the **OpenOffice.org 3.3 icon** on the desktop to open the application.
3. **Click** the **Text Document icon** to open a new document.
4. At the top of the document, **type *your name and the date and time*** that this file was created.
5. **Click File > Save As** from the toolbar.
6. In the Save As dialog box, **type Lab4 New Digital Forensic Evidence** in the File name box.
7. **Select Microsoft® Word 97/2000/XP (.doc)** from the Save as type drop-down menu, **click** the **Desktop icon**, and **click** the **Save button** to save this file to the vWorkstation desktop.

FIGURE 4.2

Saving the OpenOffice document

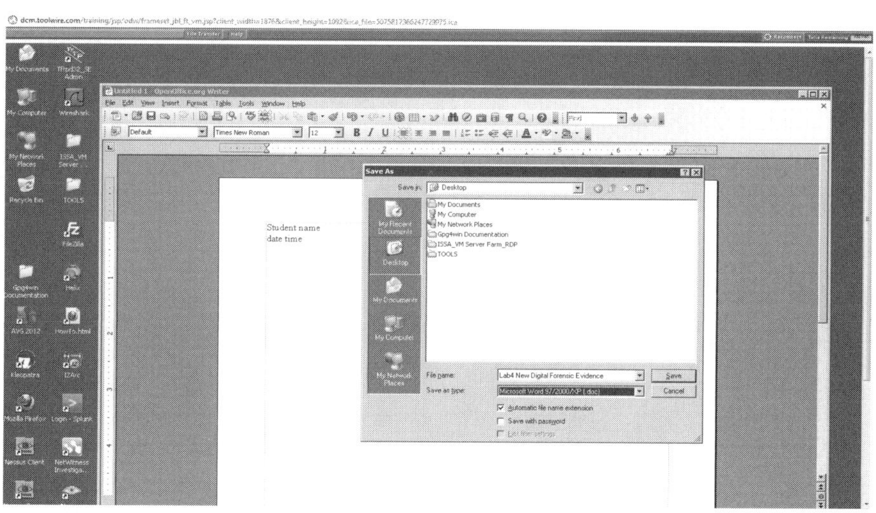

8. **Click** the **Keep Current Format button** if prompted to change the OpenOffice format type.
9. **Double-click** the **Helix icon** on the desktop to open the application.
10. **Select English** from the Choose Your Language box and **click** the **Accept button** to proceed.

    The Helix welcome screen opens with a navigation box at the left containing icons to the most common activities that forensic investigators will perform within the tool. The right pane includes a text description for each of the icons.

FIGURE 4.3

The Helix welcome screen

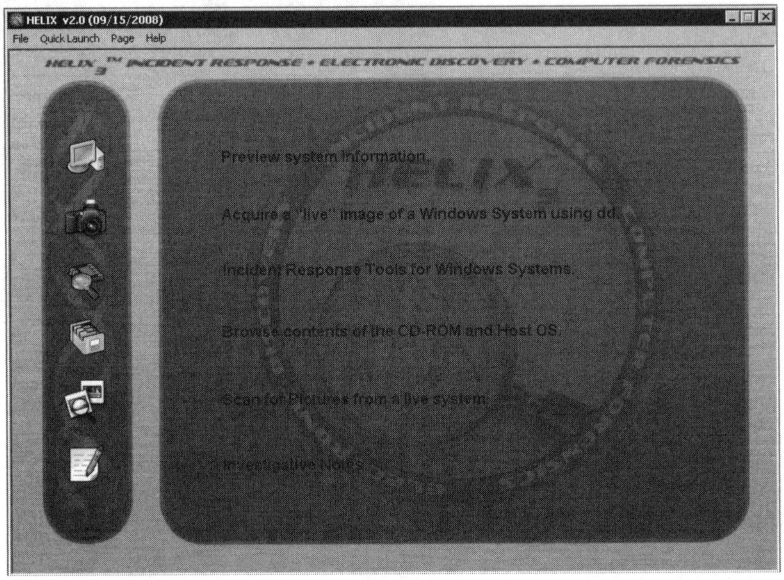

11. **Click** the **Preview system information icon** in the left navigation box.
12. **Review** the System Information screen. **Document the data** you see in the following fields in your OpenOffice file:
    - Host
    - User
    - IP
    - NIC address
    - Domain

13. **Click** the **Incident Response icon**, then **click** the **right arrow icon** between the two panes of the tool to move to the second page of the Incident Response report.

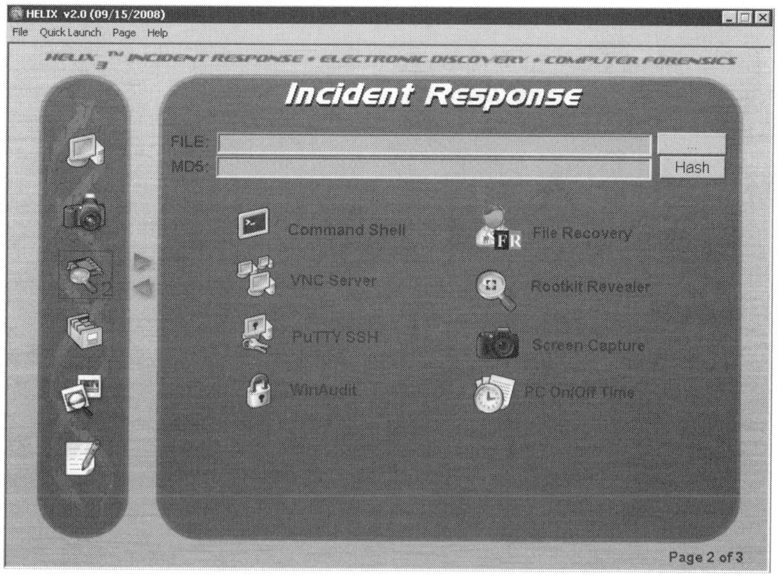

FIGURE 4.4

Page 2 of the Incident Response report

14. **Click** the **PC On/Off Time icon** and **click** the **Yes button** on the Notice pop-up to confirm you want to run the tool.

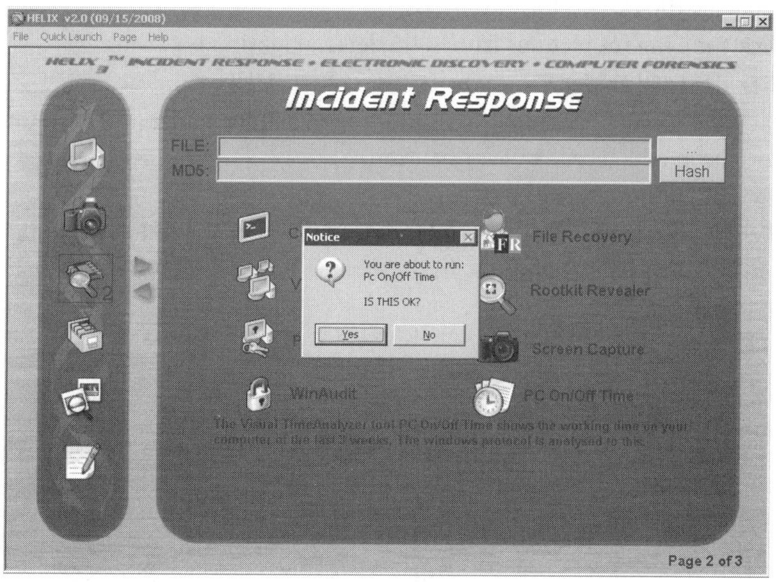

FIGURE 4.5

Starting the PC On/Off Time report

15. **Make a screen capture** of the PC On/Off Time sheet showing when the system was last turned off and on. **Paste** it into the OpenOffice text document.

> **Note:**
> To capture the screen, **press** the **Ctrl** and **PrtSc** keys together, and then **use Ctrl + V** to paste the image into a Word or other word processor document.

FIGURE 4.6

PC On/Off Time sheet

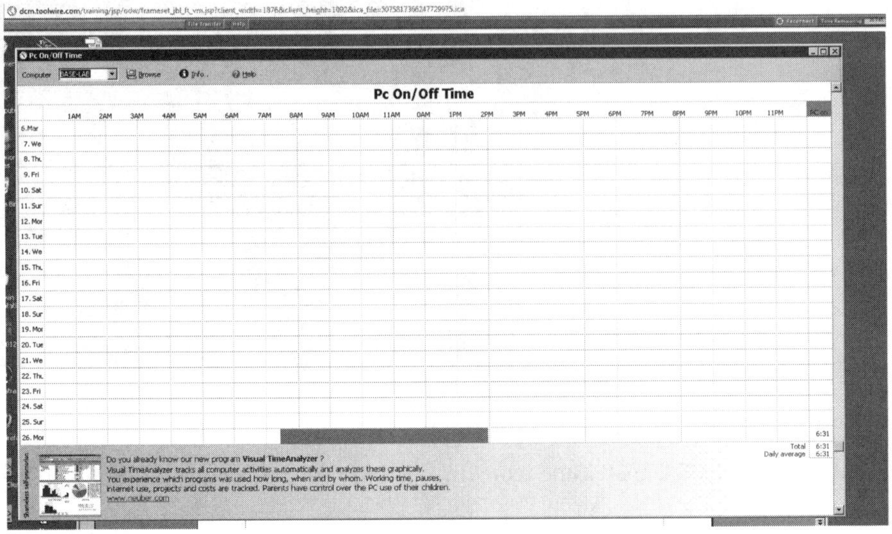

16. **Minimize** the **PC On/Off Time sheet.**
17. **Click** the **Scan for pictures icon** in the left navigation box.
18. **Click** the **Load Folder link** in the bottom of the Helix window.
19. **Navigate** to the **C:\Forensic_Tools\StegoAndSamples folder** and **click OK** to see the sample images that have been added to the vWorkstation.
20. **Click OK** in the "Please be patient" notice pop-up.
21. **Click** the **last image file** in the folder and **document the following data** (which can be found at the bottom of the Helix window) in the OpenOffice document:
    - File name
    - File size
    - Color depth

FIGURE 4.7

The StegoAndSamples folder

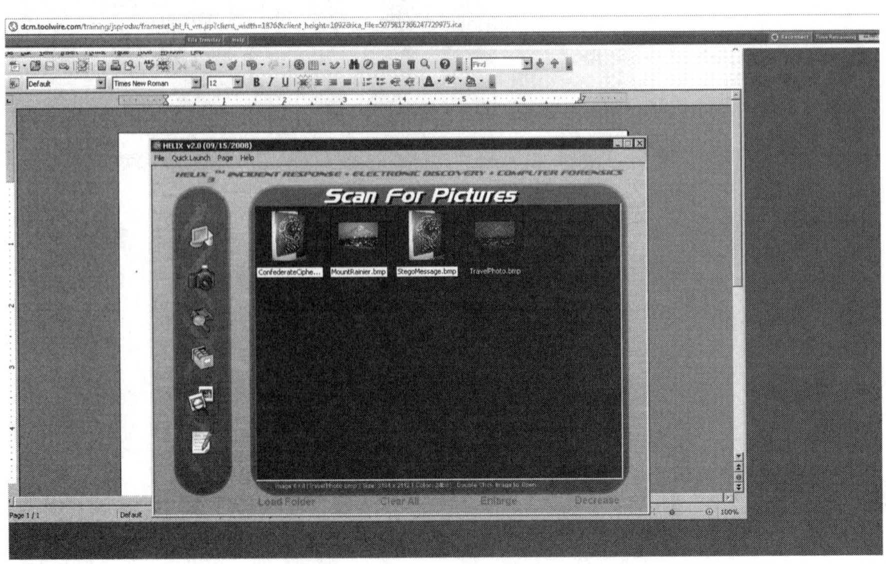

22. **Double-click** the **My Computer icon** on the vWorkstation desktop to open the Windows Explorer.
23. **Navigate** to the **C:\Forensic_Tools\StegoAndSamples folder** and find the same image.
24. **Make a screen capture** of the Windows Explorer window showing the image file's creation date and **paste** it into the OpenOffice document.
25. **Close** the **Helix window.** When you close the Helix window, it will ask if you want to save a PDF file of your actions. You can **click "No"**, as it is not needed in this lab.

> **Note:**
> The next steps will use a series of forensic tools to extract data from the Internet Explorer browser. You will document the data you find in a text document as a deliverable for this lab.

26. **Double-click** the **Internet Explorer icon** on the desktop to open the application.
27. **Minimize** the **Internet Explorer window.**
28. **Double-click** the **Tools folder** on the desktop to open the Windows Explorer.

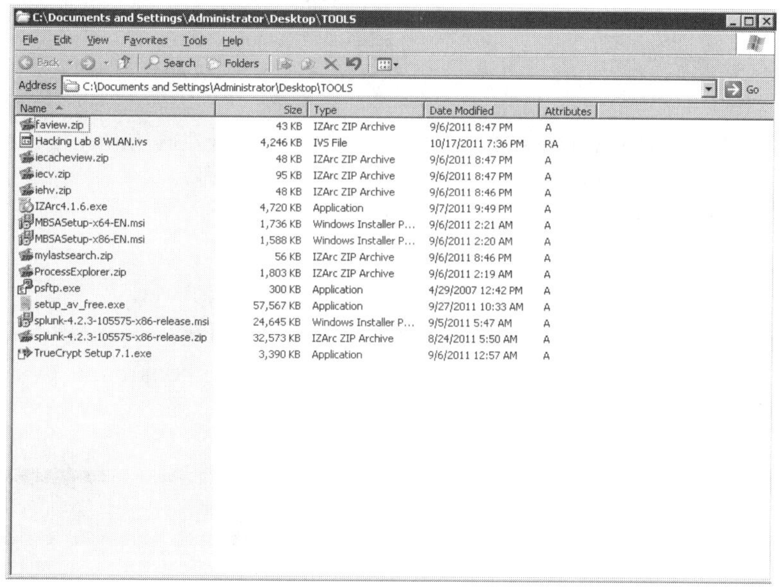

FIGURE 4.8
Windows Explorer displaying the Tools folder

29. **Double-click** the **ProcessExplorer.zip file.**
30. In the IZarc window, **double-click** the **procexp.exe file** to open the Process Explorer tool.

    More detailed than the Windows Task Manager, the Process Explorer tool displays information about currently active processes on a given machine.

31. **Click** the **iexplore.exe process** to highlight it and make note of the memory value from the Private Bytes column.

FIGURE 4.9

The Process Explorer window

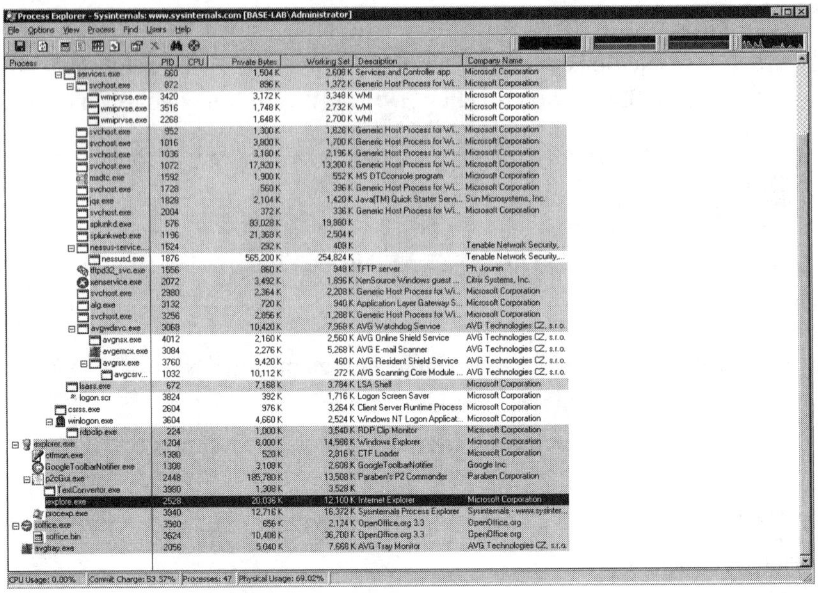

32. **Make a screen capture** of the Process Explorer window showing the iexplore.exe process data and **paste** it into the OpenOffice document.
33. **Close** the **Process Explorer window.**
34. **Close** the **IZarc window.**
35. **Double-click** the **Faview.zip file** in the Windows Explorer.
36. In the IZarc window, **double-click** the **faview.exe file** to open the FavoritesView tool.

    The FavoritesView tool displays all of a machine's bookmarks in a single page. This can make finding a specific bookmark easier.

FIGURE 4.10

The FavoritesView window

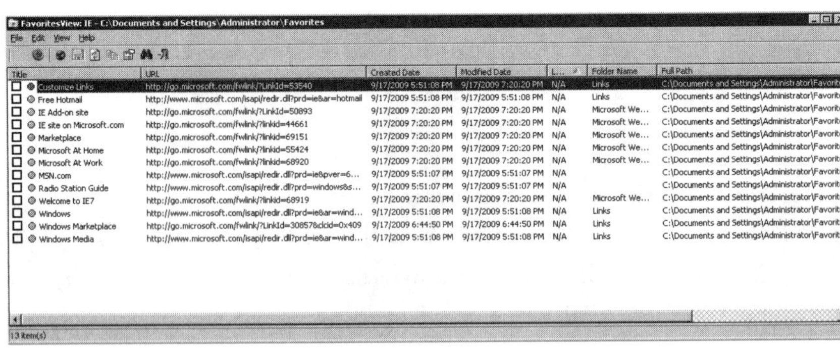

37. **Click** the **Created Date column header** to sort the list by that data point.
38. **Click** the line item with the **earliest website link visited today.**
39. With the highlighted line item visible, **make a screen capture** of the FavoritesView window and **paste** it into the OpenOffice document.
40. **Close** the **FavoritesView window.**
41. **Close** the **IZarc window.**
42. **Double-click** the **iecacheview.zip file** in the Windows Explorer.
43. In the IZarc window, **double-click** the **IECacheView.exe file** to open the IECacheView tool.

    The IECacheView tool reads the cache folder of Internet Explorer to find data about the files stored there.

44. **Click** the **Last Modified column header** to sort the list by that data point.

If the first line item displays an *N/A* in that column, click the column header again to find the most recently modified file.

45. **Click** the line item with the **most recently modified date**.

FIGURE 4.11

The IECacheView window

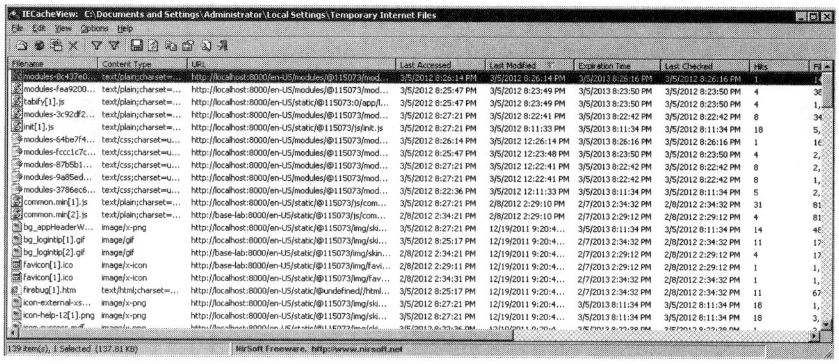

46. With the highlighted line item visible, **make a screen capture** of the IECacheView window and **paste** it into the OpenOffice document.
47. **Close** the **IECacheView window**.
48. **Close** the **IZarc window**.
49. **Double-click** the **iecv.zip file** in the Windows Explorer.
50. In the IZarc window, **double-click** the **iecv.exe file** to open the IECookiesView tool.

The IECookiesView tool displays all of the cookies stored on your machine in one page.

51. **Click** the **Hits column header** to sort the list by that data point.

If the top file in the column does not have the most hits in the list, click the column header again to find the cookies with the most hits.

52. **Click** the line item with the **most hits**.

FIGURE 4.12

The IECookiesView window

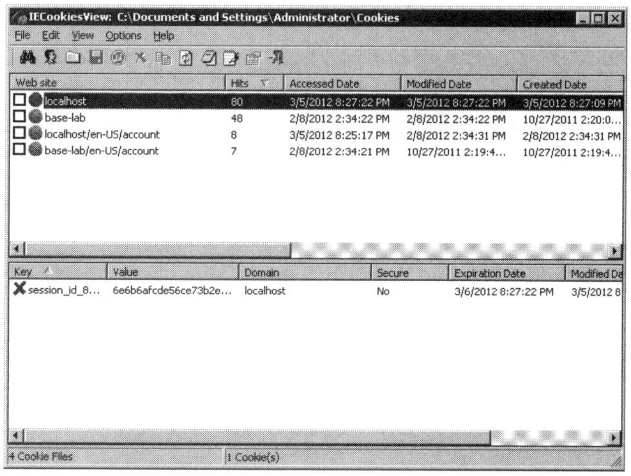

53. With the highlighted line item visible, **make a screen capture** of the IECookiesView window and **paste** it into the OpenOffice document.
54. **Close** the **IECookiesView window**.
55. **Close** the **IZarc window**.
56. **Double-click** the **iehv.zip file** in the Windows Explorer.

57. In the IZarc window, **double-click** the **iehv.exe file** to open the IEHistoryView tool.

    The IEHistoryView tool reads the browser's history file and displays all of the Internet addresses the machine has visited in recent days.

58. **Click** the **Hits column header** to sort the list by that data point.

    If the top file in the column does not have the most hits in the list, click the column header again to find the address with the most hits.

FIGURE 4.13

The IEHistoryView window

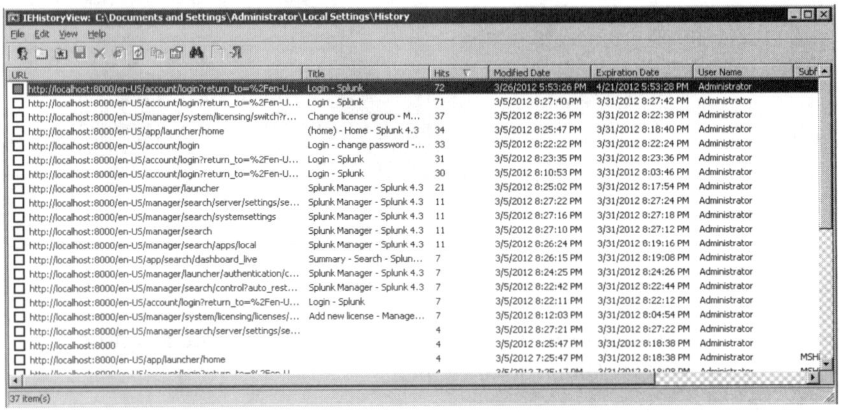

59. **Click** the line item with the **most hits**.
60. With the highlighted line item visible, **make a screen capture** of the IEHistoryView window and **paste** it into the OpenOffice document.
61. **Close** the **IEHistoryView window**.
62. **Close** the **IZarc window**.
63. **Double-click** the **mylastsearch.zip file** in the Windows Explorer.
64. In the IZarc window, **double-click** the **MyLastSearch.exe file** to open the MyLastSearch tool.

    The MyLastSearch tool displays all of the recent search queries with the most popular search engines.

65. **Click** the **Search Time column header** to sort the list by that data point.

    If the top file in the column does not have the most recent date, click the column header again to find the address with the most recent date.

66. **Click** the line item with the **most recent date**.

FIGURE 4.14

The MyLastSearch window

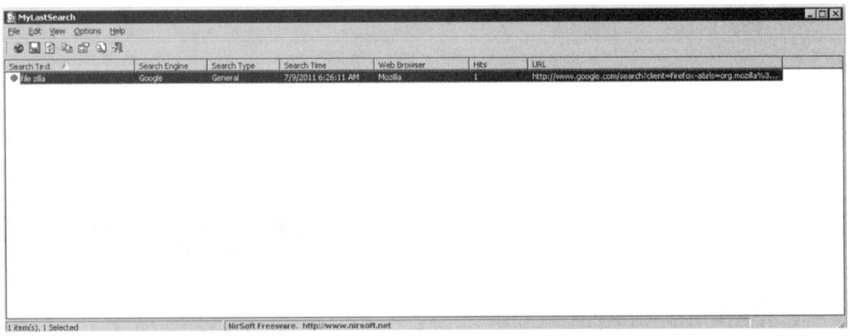

67. With the highlighted line item visible, **make a screen capture** of the MyLastSearch window and **paste** it into the OpenOffice document.
68. **Close** the **MyLastSearch window**.
69. **Close** the **IZarc window**.
70. **Close** the **Windows Explorer window**.
71. **Close** the **Internet Explorer window**.
72. **Close** the **OpenOffice.org 3.3 window** and **click Yes** when prompted to save your changes.
73. Use the **File Transfer button** to download the **Lab4 New Digital Forensic Evidence** to your local computer and submit it as part of your deliverables.

Evaluation Criteria and Rubrics

The following are the evaluation criteria and rubrics for Lab #4 that the students must perform:

1. Was the student able to load and run the Helix bootable utilities application? – [**20%**]
2. Was the student able to use the Helix utilities to identify system state and potential evidence in a forensically sound manner while working with a running system? – [**20%**]
3. Was the student able to apply a variety of utilities to identify data of potential evidentiary value while sustaining the state of the system and preserving forensic integrity? – [**20%**]
4. Was the student able to identify which forensic evidence or investigation tool can be used to conduct various forensic investigations that can be submitted as evidence in a court of law? – [**20%**]
5. Was the student able to create a report presenting details of running processes and browser usage for the landing vWorkstation? – [**20%**]

LAB #4 – ASSESSMENT WORKSHEET

Uncover New Digital Evidence Using Bootable Utilities

Course Name and Number: _______________

Student Name: _______________

Instructor Name: _______________

Lab Due Date: _______________

Overview

Any time forensic investigators explore a machine in search of evidence, they risk changing the very data they seek, potentially invalidating evidence. For this reason, they make use of tools that incorporate write-blocking technologies. The VSCL uses an image of an evidence drive to perform an investigation. In this lab, you loaded various forensic applications and tools and ran them locally on the target workstation or server under investigation. You became familiar with the features and functions of the forensic applications in this lab: FavoritesView, IECacheView, IECookiesView, IEHistoryView, Helix, MyLastSearch, and Process Explorer.

Lab Assessment Questions & Answers

1. What is the main advantage of a bootable forensic suite like Helix?

____

2. Describe five Process Explorer features that can be used in computer forensics as part of an investigation.

____

3. Which forensics tool would you use to reveal recent pages viewed via the Internet Explorer browser?

____

____

____

____

4. How would IECacheView help a forensic investigator?

____

____

____

____

5. All of the tools used in this lab are intended to analyze data. What is the difference between data and evidence?

____

____

____

____

Automate Digital Evidence Discovery Using Paraben's P2 Commander

LAB 5

Introduction

Any time forensic investigators explore a machine in search of evidence, they risk changing the very data they seek, potentially invalidating evidence. For this reason, they make use of tools that incorporate write-blocking technologies. The VSCL uses an image of an evidence drive to perform an investigation. In this lab, you will use Paraben's P2 Commander to load and sort evidence file types, analyze an image of a partition drive, and identify potential evidentiary information by examining chat logs, Skype sessions, and e-mails.

Learning Objectives

Upon completing this lab, you will be able to:

- Load and sort evidence file types in a case using Paraben's P2 Commander forensic tool
- Locate an image of a partition drive and analyze the data on the image and the files saved in the evidence drive and new case file
- Use P2 Commander to identify information for potential evidence contained in chat logs, such as Skype chat or Eudora e-mail messages
- Analyze the contents of user profiles, data, chat logs, and e-mails using the P2 Commander
- Craft a new evidence report of your findings and ensure that it conforms to the chain of custody with each step and task performed with a corresponding date and timestamp

TOOLS AND SOFTWARE

NAME	MORE INFORMATION
P2 Commander	http://www.paraben.com/p2-commander.html

Deliverables

Upon completion of this lab, you are required to provide the following deliverables to your instructor:

1. A text document containing screen captures of the following:
   a. The number of files in specified type categories;
   b. The final Eudora e-mail outbox showing the text of the first e-mail message;
2. Lab #5 Digital Forensic Case File.p2c;
3. Lab Assessment Questions & Answers for Lab #5 .

Hands-On Steps

1. This lab begins at the student landing vWorkstation virtual machine desktop of the VSCL, as shown here.

FIGURE 5.1

"Student Landing" VSCL workstation

> **Note:**
> The next steps will create a new case file using Paraben's P2 Commander. You will load and sort digital evidence. You will record the information you uncover as a deliverable for this lab.

2. **Double-click** the **OpenOffice.org 3.3 icon** on the desktop to open the application.
3. **Click** the **Text Document icon** to open a new document.
4. At the top of the document, **type *your name and the date and time*** that this file was created.
5. **Click File > Save As** from the toolbar.
6. In the Save As dialog box, **type Lab5 Digital Evidence Case File Report** in the File name box.
7. **Select Microsoft® Word 97/2000/XP (.doc)** from the Save as type drop-down menu, **click** the **Desktop icon**, and **click** the **Save button** to save this file to the vWorkstation desktop.

FIGURE 5.2

Saving the OpenOffice document

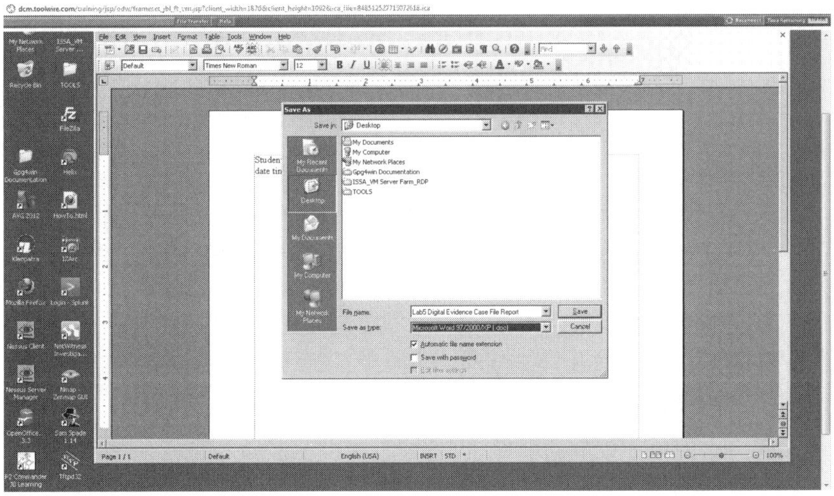

8. **Click** the **Keep Current Format button** if prompted to change the OpenOffice format type.
9. **Double-click** the **P2 Commander JB Learning icon** on the desktop to open the application.

   The P2 Commander's welcome screen opens with a navigation box entitled *Start your work here* at the left containing links to the most common activities that forensic investigators will perform within the tool.
10. **Click** the **Create new case link** in the left navigation box.

FIGURE 5.3

The P2 Commander welcome screen

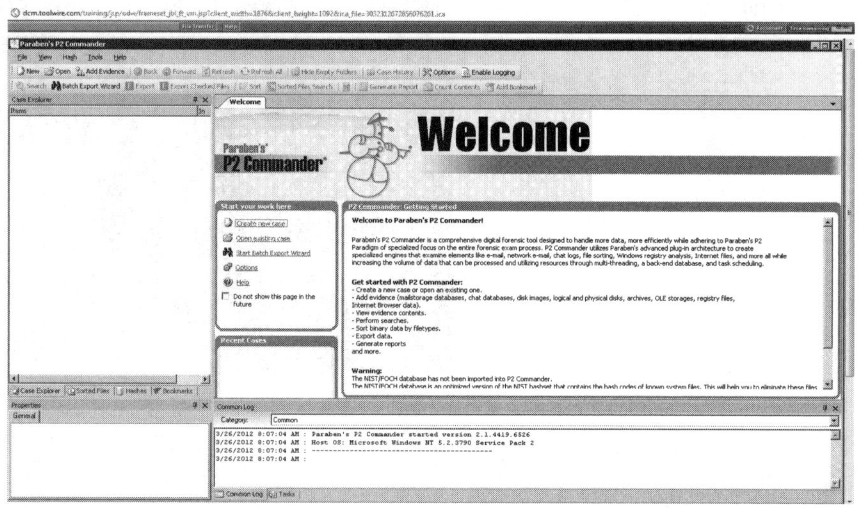

11. In the New Case dialog box, **click** the **Case Properties tab**.
12. **Type Lab #5 Digital Forensic Case File** in the Case name box.

FIGURE 5.4

The New Case dialog box

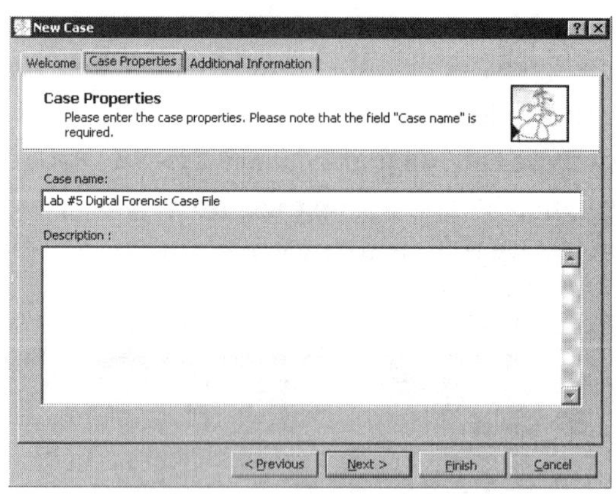

13. **Click** the **Additional Information tab** to continue.
14. **Type** ***your name*** in the Investigator's name box and **click** the **Finish button**.
15. In the New case creation dialog box, **type Lab #5 Digital Forensic Case File** in the File name box, if necessary.

16. **Click Save** to create the new case file.

    A Lab #5 Digital Forensic Case File tab is added to the P2 Commander screen and the Add New Evidence dialog box opens.

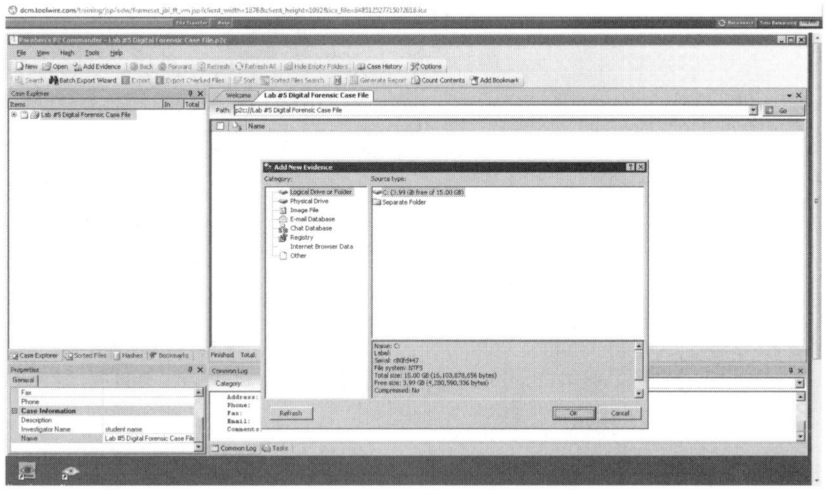

FIGURE 5.5

The Add New Evidence dialog box

17. **Click Image File** in the left pane of the Add New Evidence dialog box.
18. **Click Drive image** in the right pane and **click OK**.

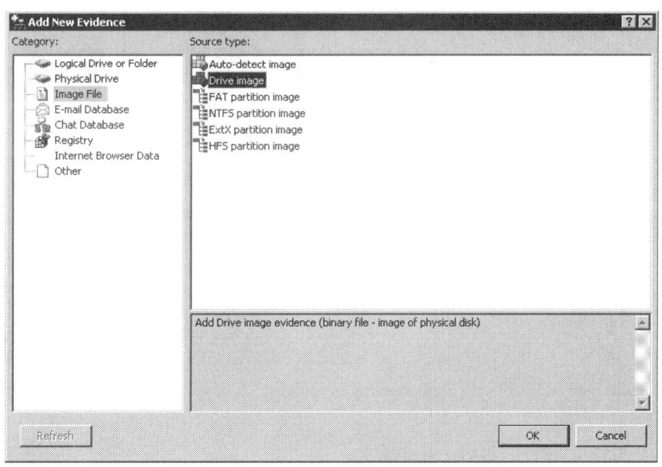

FIGURE 5.6

Adding evidence to the case file

19. In the Open dialog box, **navigate** to the **C:\Forensic_Tools\vm_image folder**, **select** the **evidence_drive.e01.E01 file**, and **click Open**.

20. In the Enter a new evidence name box, **type Lab #5 Forensic Analysis** and **click OK** to add the data from this file to your case file.

FIGURE 5.7

Identifying the digital image file

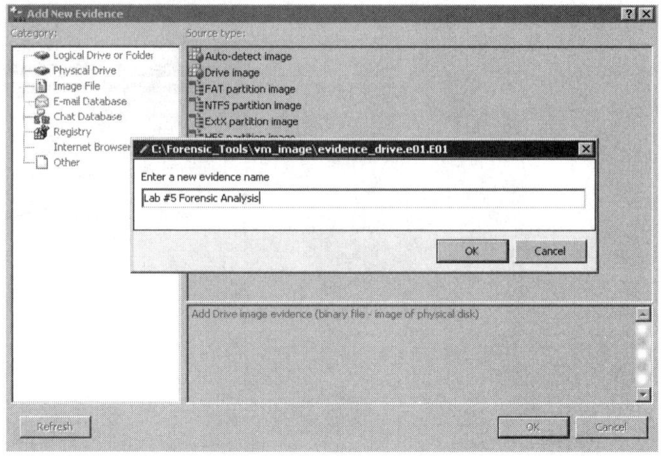

21. **Double-click Lab #5 Forensic Analysis** in the right pane of the P2 Commander.
22. **Double-click Partition Parser**.
23. **Double-click Partition0**.

    The NTFS dialog box will pop up.
24. **Verify** that all options in the NTFS Settings dialog box are checked and **click OK**.

FIGURE 5.8

NTFS Settings dialog box

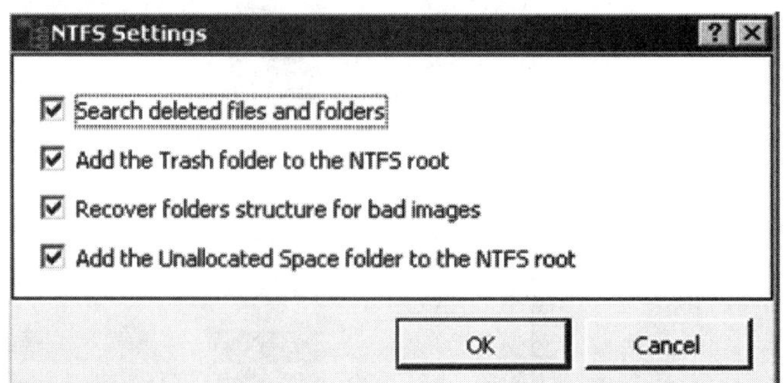

25. **Double-click NTFS** in the right pane.
26. **Double-click** the **Root folder** to see the file structure of the evidence image.
27. **Click** the **Lab #5 Digital Forensic Case File folder** in the left Case Explorer pane.
28. **Right-click Lab #5 Forensic Analysis** in the right pane and **select Sorting** from the context menu.

29. **Accept** the **default selections** in the P2 Commander Sorting Engine and **click Finish**.

    This process will take several minutes. When it is finished, the Completed tab in the bottom pane of the P2 Commander window will show at (1) indicator.

FIGURE 5.9

P2 Commander Sorting Engine

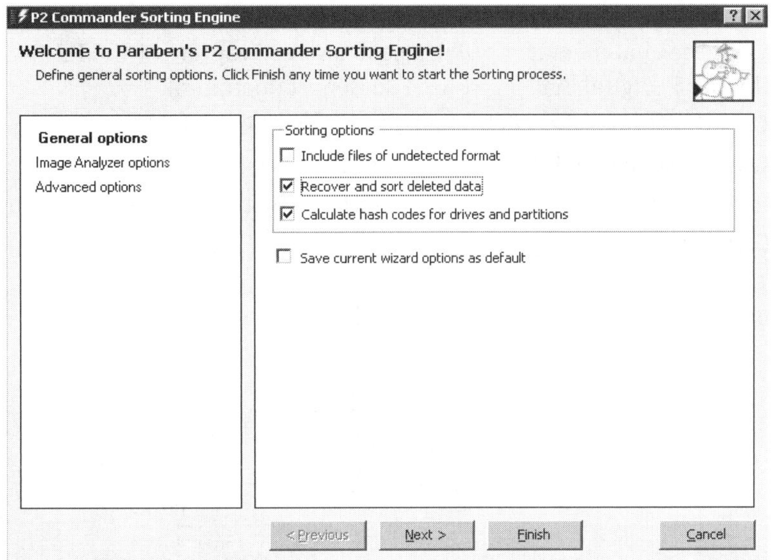

30. **Click** the **Sorted Files tab** in the bottom left pane of the P2 Commander window.

    All of the files that P2 Commander reviewed will appear in the right pane. The Sorted Files tab in this pane displays the number of files that were sorted.

31. With the number of sorted files visible, **make a screen capture** of the P2 Commander window and **paste** it into the Lab5 Digital Evidence Case File Report document.

> **Note:**
>
> To capture the screen, **press** the **Ctrl** and **PrtSc** keys together, and then **use Ctrl + V** to paste the image into a Word or other word processor document.

32. **Double-click** the **Sorted Files item** in the left pane and **click Chats** to load information about Skype usage on this machine.

FIGURE 5.10

P2 Commander Chats data

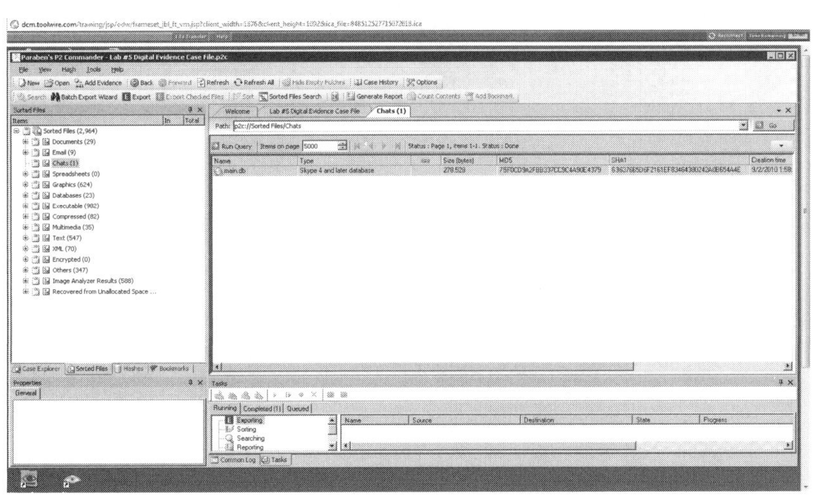

33. In the right-pane, **double-click main.db** to open to the relevant Skype files.
34. **Scroll** down the **Text Pane** in the bottom right pane to find a chat conversation between badguy11111 and badguy22222.

    Use the scrollbar at the right of the Text Pane and scroll slowly until you see these user names. Review the message you see there.
35. With the chat messages visible, **make a screen capture** of the P2 Commander window and **paste** it into the Lab5 Digital Evidence Case File Report document.
36. **Click** the **Sorted Files tab** in the bottom left pane of the P2 Commander window.
37. **Click Email** to load information about the Eudora e-mail usage on this machine.
38. In the right-pane, **double-click Out.mbx** to start the process of reading the e-mail file.
39. **Click Yes** when prompted to mount the Folder Eudora as a database.

    This process takes a very long time. When completed the right pane of the P2 Commander will list the outgoing e-mail messages that have been stored in this machine.

FIGURE 5.11

Eudora database prompt

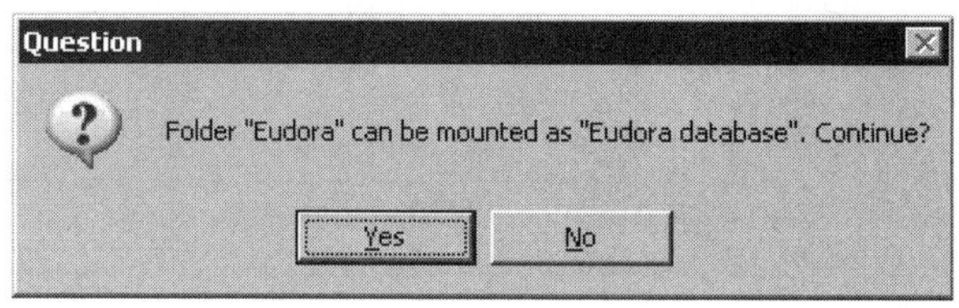

40. **Click Eudora database** to open to the Eudora e-mail folders.

FIGURE 5.12

Open the Eudora Outbox

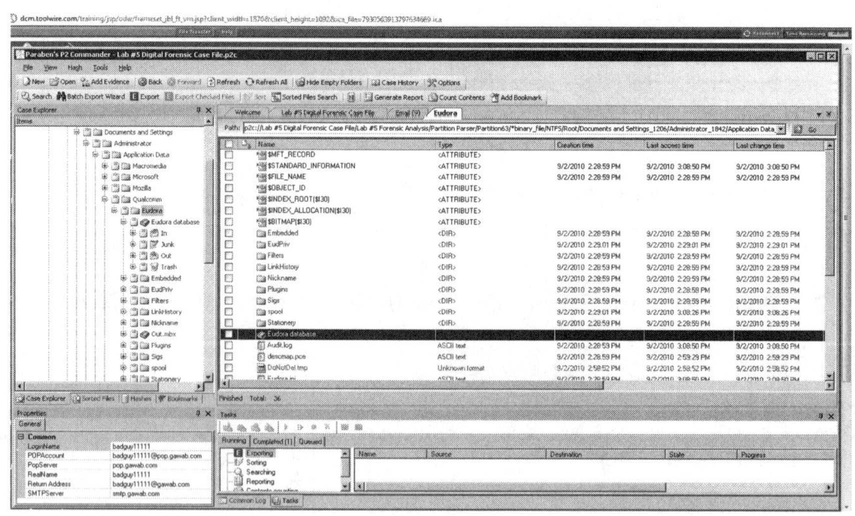

41. **Double-click** the **Out folder** to view the Outbox.

FIGURE 5.13

Eudora Outbox in the P2 Commander

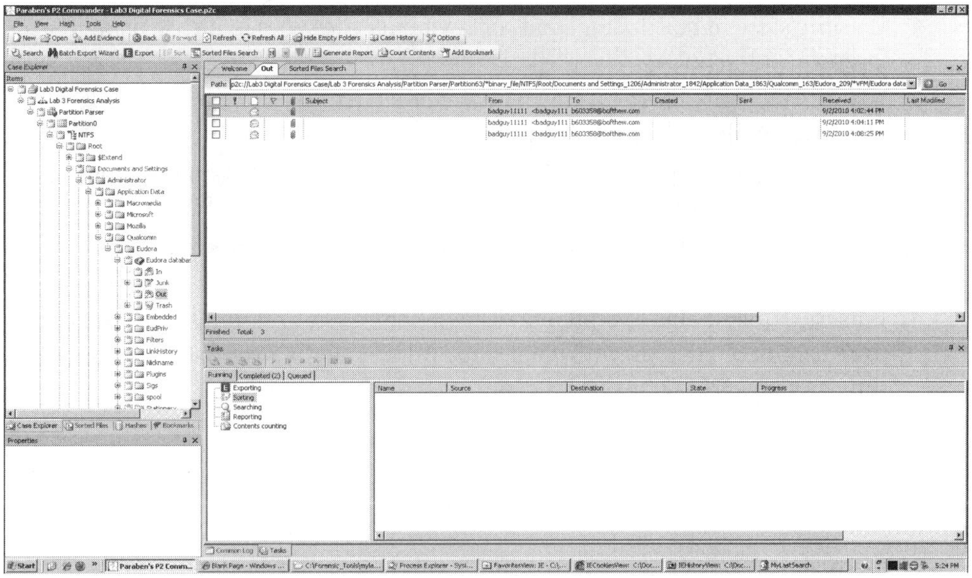

42. **Double-click** the **first e-mail** in the list and view the content in the E-mail Data pane at the bottom right of the P2 Commander window.

    Drag the border between the details pane and the E-mail Data pane up to view the entire contents of the message.

43. With the text for the first e-mail still visible, **make a screen capture** of the P2 Commander window and **paste** it into the Lab5 Digital Evidence Case File Report document.
44. **Close** the **OpenOffice.org 3.3 window** and **click Yes** when prompted to save your changes.
45. **Close** the **P2 Commander window**.
46. Use the **File Transfer button** to download the **text file** to your local computer and submit it as part of your deliverables.

Evaluation Criteria and Rubrics

The following are the evaluation criteria and rubrics for Lab #5 that the students must perform:

1. Was the student able to load and sort evidence file types in a case using Paraben's P2 Commander forensic tool? – [**20%**]
2. Was the student able to locate an image of a partition drive and analyze the data on the image and the files saved in the evidence drive and new case file? – [**20%**]
3. Was the student able to use P2 Commander to identify information for potential evidence contained in chat logs, such as Skype chat or Eudora e-mail messages? – [**20%**]
4. Was the student able to analyze the contents of user profiles, data, chat logs, and e-mails using the P2 Commander? – [**20%**]
5. Was the student able to craft a new evidence report of findings and ensure that it conforms to the chain of custody with each step and task performed with a corresponding date and timestamp? – [**20%**]

LAB #5 – ASSESSMENT WORKSHEET

Automate Digital Evidence Discovery Using Paraben's P2 Commander

Course Name and Number: ______________________________

Student Name: ______________________________

Instructor Name: ______________________________

Lab Due Date: ______________________________

Overview

Any time forensic investigators explore a machine in search of evidence, they risk changing the very data they seek, potentially invalidating evidence. For this reason, they make use of tools that incorporate write-blocking technologies. The VSCL uses an image of an evidence drive to perform an investigation. In this lab, you used Paraben's P2 Commander to load and sort evidence file types, analyze an image of a partition drive, and identify potential evidentiary information by examining chat logs, Skype sessions, and e-mails.

Lab Assessment Questions & Answers

1. Why did you have to drill down within the file directory structure drives, directories, sub-directories, and folders within P2 Commander when building the new case file?

____

____

____

____

2. List at least five file types/categories that P2 Commander sorts when building a new evidence case file of an evidence hard drive.

____

____

____

____

3. What type of IM CHAT was identified by P2 Commander on the evidence hard drive under investigation?

4. Were the images (i.e., graphics, photos, pictures, etc.) still visible on the evidence hard drive under investigation? What about those that were put in the workstation trash bin?

5. What was the e-mail application used by this particular user on the evidence hard drive under investigation?

Apply Steganography to Uncover Modifications to an Image File

LAB 6

Introduction

Any time forensic investigators explore a machine in search of evidence, they risk changing the very data they seek, potentially invalidating evidence. For this reason, they make use of tools that incorporate write-blocking technologies. The VSCL uses an image of an evidence drive to perform an investigation. In this lab, you will use S-Tools and the Windows Picture and Fax Viewer to discover possible forensic steganographic activity (the act of secreting files or other potentially harmful data—or payloads—within another file, in this case image files). You will also properly identify and extract embedded data in a carrier image.

Learning Objectives

Upon completing this lab, you will be able to:

- Use the S-Tools for Windows utility to search for possible steganographic activity embedded in image files
- Extract a cipher key text file
- Identify the use of steganographic data concealment techniques for covert communication and potential injected data
- Extract steganographically sequestered data from identified image files while conserving their integrity
- Report the details of hidden files

TOOLS AND SOFTWARE	
NAME	**MORE INFORMATION**
S-Tools	http://www.spychecker.com/program/stools.html
Windows Picture and Fax Viewer	http://www.microsoft.com/resources/documentation/windows/xp/all/proddocs/en-us/image_overview.mspx

Deliverables

Upon completion of this lab, you are required to provide the following deliverables to your instructor:

1. A text document containing each of the following:
   a. File names, sizes, and a one-sentence description of the images specified in this lab;
   b. The contents of the extracted cipher key text file;
   c. File name and encryption algorithm used to reveal hidden files in the images;
   d. File names, sizes, and a one-sentence description of the contents of each extracted file;
   e. Comparison between source image size and the total combined file sizes of the steganographically combined carrier and payload files;
2. Lab Assessment Questions & Answers for Lab #6.

Hands-On Steps

1. This lab begins at the student landing vWorkstation virtual machine desktop of the VSCL, as shown here.

FIGURE 6.1

"Student Landing" VSCL workstation

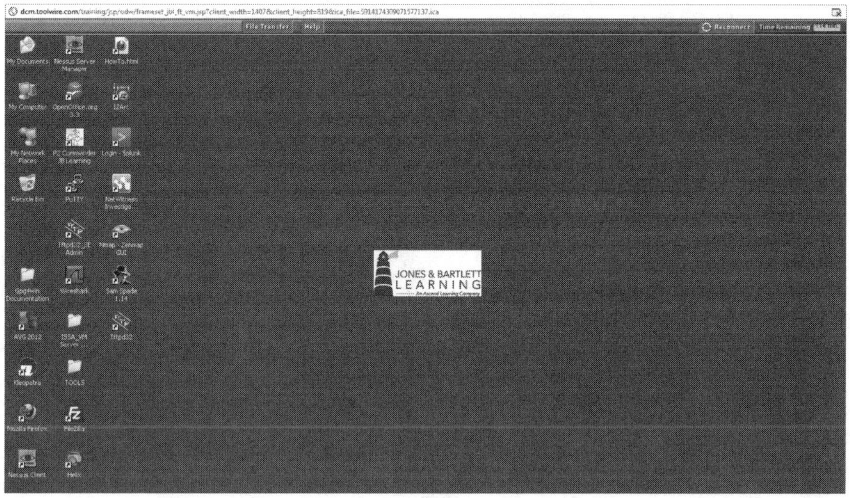

> **Note:**
> The next steps will use the S-Tools application to check the image files on the vWorkstation desktop for possible steganographic activity. You will record the information you uncover as a deliverable for this lab.

2. **Double-click** the **OpenOffice.org 3.3 icon** on the desktop to open the application.
3. **Click** the **Text Document icon** to open a new document.
4. At the top of the document, **type *your name and the date and time*** that this file was created.
5. **Click File > Save As** from the toolbar.
6. In the Save As dialog box, **type Lab #6 Steganography Documentation Report** in the File name box.
7. **Select Microsoft® Word 97/2000/XP (.doc)** from the Save as type drop-down menu, **click** the **Desktop icon**, and **click** the **Save button** to save this file to the vWorkstation desktop.

FIGURE 6.2

Saving the OpenOffice document

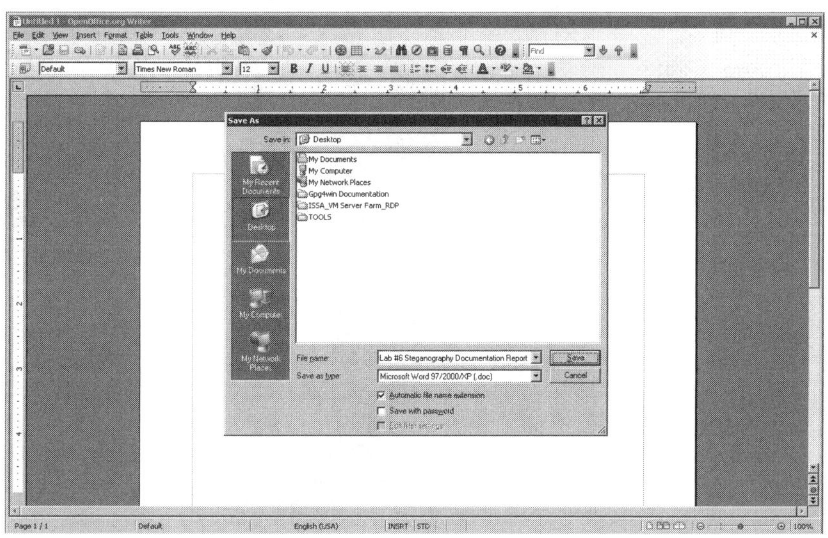

8. **Click** the **Keep Current Format button** if prompted to change the OpenOffice format type.
9. **Double-click** the **My Computer icon** on the desktop to open the Windows Explorer.
10. **Double-click** the **Local Disk (C:) folder**.
11. **Double-click** the **Forensic_Tools folder**.
12. **Double-click** the **StegoAndSamples folder**.
13. **Hold** the **CTRL key** and **click** each of the following image files:
    - ConfederateCipher.bmp
    - MountRainier.bmp
    - StegoMessage.bmp
    - TravelPhoto.bmp

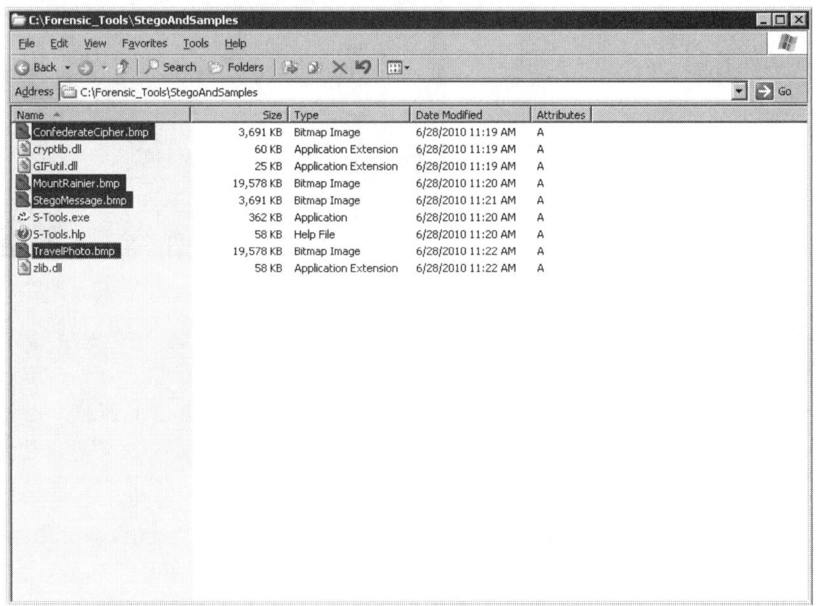

FIGURE 6.3

Selecting the images for review

14. With the mouse pointer over one of the highlighted images, **right-click Open with** and **select Windows Picture and Fax Viewer** from the context menu.

    The four images will open in the Windows Picture and Fax Viewer. Below the image is a toolbar for the application that includes previous and next arrows, zoom controls, and editing tools.

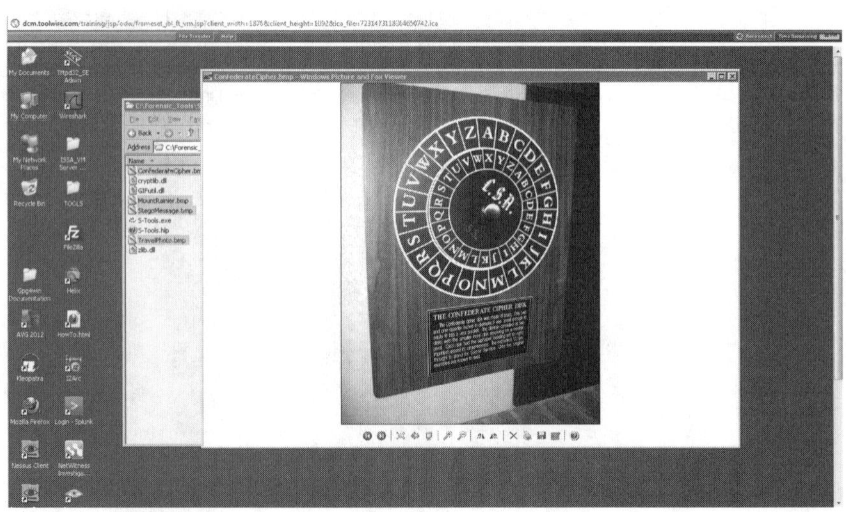

FIGURE 6.4

The Windows Picture and Fax Viewer

15. **Review** the image files in both the Windows Explorer and the Windows Picture and Fax Viewer (the Viewer). **Document** the following information for each image in your text document:
    - File name
    - File size
    - One-sentence description of the image you see in the Viewer
16. **Click** the **Viewer**.
17. In the Windows Explorer, **double-click** the **S-Tools.exe file** to open the application.
18. **Click Continue** to bypass the option to review the application's quick start guide.
19. Adjust the sizes of the open windows so that the Windows Explorer and the S-Tools utility are both visible.
20. **Drag StegoMessage.bmp** from the Windows Explorer and **drop** it into the **S-Tools window**.

FIGURE 6.5
Viewing the StegoMessage.bmp file in S-Tools

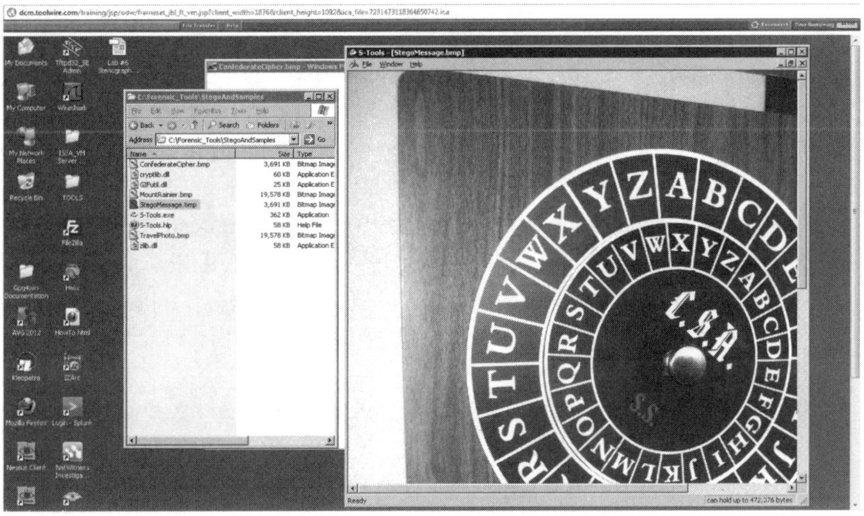

21. **Right-click** the **StegoMessage.bmp** in the S-Tools utility and **select Reveal** from the context menu.
22. In the Revealing from StegoMessage.bmp dialog box, **type** the **abcd** in both the Passphrase and Verify passphrase boxes.
23. Accept the default encryption algorithm, IDEA, and **click OK**.

    The S-Tools utility reveals two files (Cipherkey.txt and Loremipsum.txt) in a new Revealed Archive window. The file size for each embedded payload file is also displayed.
24. In the Lab #6 Steganography Documentation Report, **document** the **encryption algorithm** used to reveal these files.

> **Note:**
> The hidden files are encrypted using an encryption algorithm. S-Tools uses four common encryption algorithms. You will test each encryption algorithm on all of the images in this lab as described in the following steps. Of course, not all image files will include hidden files. If no files are revealed, proceed to the next image.

25. **Right-click** the **Cipherkey.txt** in the S-Tools utility and **select Save as** from the context menu.

FIGURE 6.6

Selecting the Cipherkey

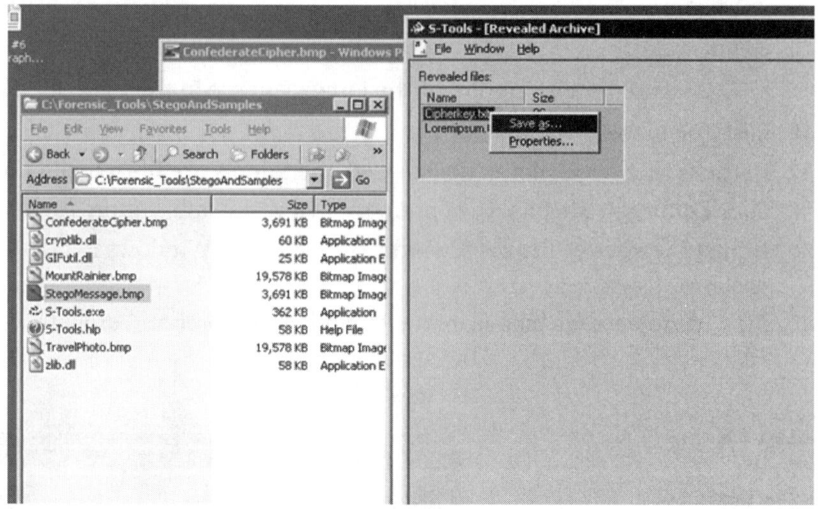

26. Accept all of the defaults in the Save As dialog box and **click Save** to save the file in the My Documents folder.
27. **Click** the **My Documents icon** on the vWorkstation desktop to open that folder in the Windows Explorer.
28. **Double-click** the **Cipherkey.txt** to open the extracted file.

    The file includes two entries: *Cipher Key* and *Message* followed by a string of letters. The message is the encrypted payload inserted into the image file. The cipher key is the decryption code needed to read the message.
29. In the Lab #6 Steganography Documentation Report, **document** the following information for the extracted file:
    - File name (from the Revealed Archive window of S-Tools)
    - File size (from the Revealed Archive window of S-Tools)
    - Brief description of the extracted file (for instance, cipher key, Lorem ipsum text, black cat, or similar description)
30. **Copy** the cipher key and message text and **paste** it into the Lab #6 Steganography Documentation Report. Note this item is only required if a cipherkey.txt file is revealed by S-Tools.
31. **Close** the **extracted file**.
32. **Repeat steps 25-30** for any other file(s) revealed by S-Tools.
33. In the Lab #6 Steganography Documentation Report, **add** the **total file size** of the payload files (in this case, Cipherkey.txt and Loremipsum.txt) and **document the total**.
34. **Compare** that total with the file size of the source image recorded in step 15 and **document your observations** in the Lab #6 Steganography Documentation Report.
35. **Close** the **Revealed Archive window** in the S-Tools utility.
36. **Close** the **StegoMessage.bmp window** in the S-Tools utility.
37. **Repeat steps 20-35** for each of the image files identified in step 13 using the following encryption algorithms:
    - Review **ConfederateCipher.bmp** using the **DES** algorithm
    - Review **MountRainier.bmp** using the **MDC** algorithm
    - Review **TravelPhoto.bmp** using the **TripleDES** algorithm
38. **Close** the **OpenOffice.org 3.3 window** and **click Yes** when prompted to save your changes.
39. **Close** the **S-Tools window**.
40. Use the **File Transfer button** to download the **Lab #6 Steganography Documentation Report** to your local computer and submit it as part of your deliverables.

Evaluation Criteria and Rubrics

The following are the evaluation criteria and rubrics for Lab #6 that the students must perform:

1. Was the student able to use the S-Tools for Windows utility to search for possible steganographic activity embedded in image files? – [**20%**]
2. Was the student able to extract a cipher key text file? – [**20%**]
3. Was the student able to identify the use of steganographic data concealment techniques for covert communication and potential injected data? – [**20%**]
4. Was the student able to extract steganographically sequestered data from identified image files while conserving their integrity? – [**20%**]
5. Was the student able to report the details of hidden files? – [**20%**]

LAB #6 – ASSESSMENT WORKSHEET

Apply Steganography to Uncover Modifications to an Image File

Course Name and Number: _______________

Student Name: _______________

Instructor Name: _______________

Lab Due Date: _______________

Overview

Any time forensic investigators explore a machine in search of evidence, they risk changing the very data they seek, potentially invalidating evidence. For this reason, they make use of tools that incorporate write-blocking technologies. The VSCL uses an image of an evidence drive to perform an investigation. In this lab, you used S-Tools and the Windows Picture and Fax Viewer to discover possible forensic steganographic activity within the sample image files provided. You also properly identified and extracted embedded data in a carrier image.

Lab Assessment Questions & Answers

1. What is steganography?

____

____

____

____

2. Describe a legitimate business need to leverage steganography.

____

____

____

____

3. What is the difference between steganography and cryptography? Why are they so important in information systems security? Explain.

4. What were the names and sizes of the two hidden text files that you uncovered using S-Tools on the "StegoMessage.bmp" image file?

5. What is the value of the cipher key?

Decode an FTP Protocol Session and Perform Forensic Analysis

LAB 7

Introduction

In this lab, you will capture data using Wireshark and explore the forensic capabilities of NetWitness Investigator using the sample protocol capture files provided. You will identify cleartext logon communications and IP hosts as well as network devices. You also will use NetWitness Investigator to analyze the difference between network cleartext and encrypted communications.

Learning Objectives

Upon completing this lab, you will be able to:

- Perform forensic protocol analysis on an FTP protocol capture
- Examine, at the protocol level, client and server FTP communications using cleartext
- Capture and identify logon credentials unencrypted as part of a forensic investigation
- Identify FTP client and server TCP/IP communications and dialogue, including three-way handshake and FTP file transfer
- Compare Wireshark and NetWitness Investigator as a forensic analysis tool for protocol capture and analysis

TOOLS AND SOFTWARE	
NAME	MORE INFORMATION
NetWitness Investigator	http://www.emc.com/security/rsa-netwitness.htm
Wireshark	http://www.wireshark.org/

Deliverables

Upon completion of this lab, you are required to provide the following deliverables to your instructor:

1. A text document that includes the following content:
   a. Screen capture of the initial "ftpcapture.pcap" import into Wireshark;
   b. Screen capture of the initial "ftpcapture.pcap" import into NetWitness Investigator;
   c. The logon IDs and password combinations used during this lab;
2. Lab Assessment Questions & Answers for Lab #7.

Hands-On Steps

1. This lab begins at the student landing vWorkstation virtual machine desktop of the VSCL, as shown here.

FIGURE 7.1
"Student Landing" VSCL workstation

> **Note:**
> The next steps will use the Wireshark utility to examine a protocol capture and find specific information needed to complete the deliverables for this lab.

2. **Double-click** the **Wireshark icon** on the desktop to open the application.

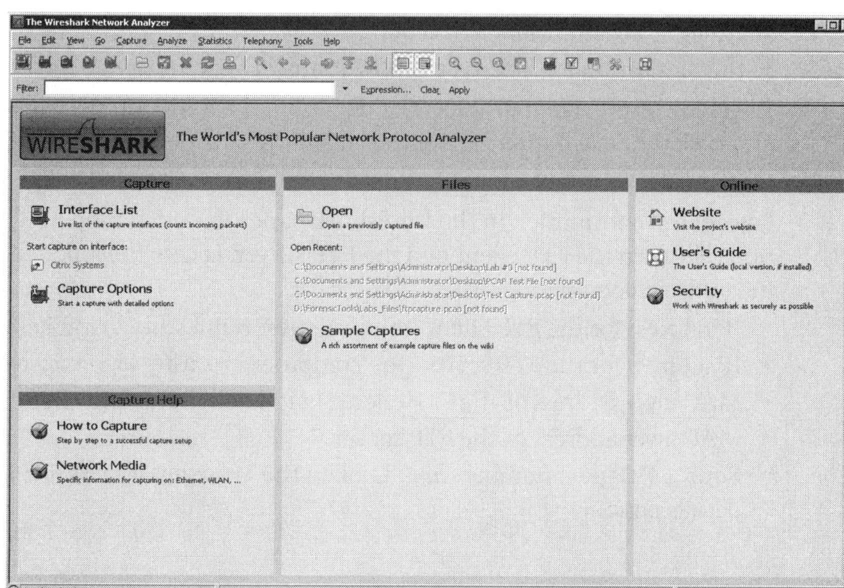

FIGURE 7.2
The Wireshark application

3. **Click File > Open** from the Wireshark toolbar.
4. In the Open dialog box, **click** the **My Computer icon**.
5. **Double-click** the **Local Drive (C:) icon**.
6. **Double-click** the **Security_Strategies folder**.
7. **Double-click** the **SystemForensics folder**.
8. **Click** the **ftpcapture.pcap file** to select it and **click Open**.

   The packet information is shown in the three panes of the Wireshark application. As you highlight items in the Packet list pane, further information is provided in the Packet details pane.

FIGURE 7.3

ftpcapture.pcap in the Wireshark window

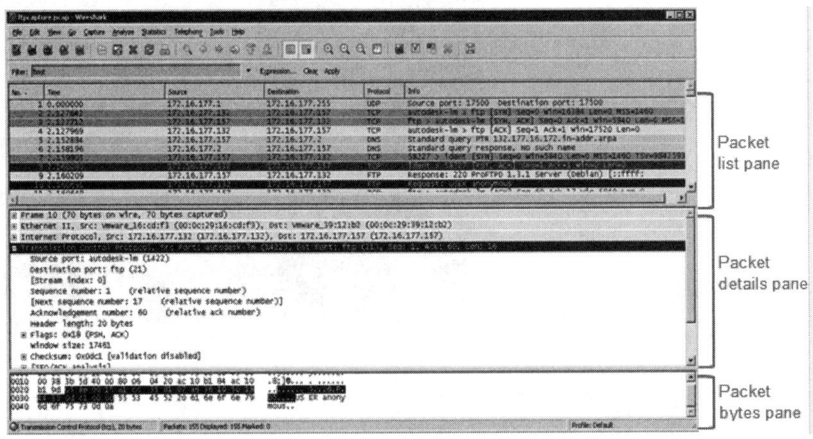

9. **Drag** the **border** between the Packet list pane and the Packet details pane to expand the size of the details pane. This will help you find the information you need for this lab.
10. **Double-click** the **OpenOffice.org 3.3 icon** on the desktop to open the application.
11. **Click** the **Text Document icon** to open a new document.
12. At the top of the document, **type *your name and the date and time*** that this file was created.
13. **Click File > Save As** from the toolbar.
14. In the Save As dialog box, **type Lab #7 Protocol Analysis** in the File name box.
15. **Select Microsoft® Word 97/2000/XP (.doc)** from the Save as type drop-down menu, **click** the **Desktop icon**, and **click** the **Save button** to save this file to the vWorkstation desktop.
16. **Click** the **Keep Current Format button** if prompted to change the OpenOffice format type.
17. **Review** the information in the Wireshark panes to understand how Wireshark presents communications between the FTP client and the FTP server. **Locate** the following items and **record** the information in your text document:
    - IP address for the FTP client (the computer requesting logon access)
    - IP address for the FTP server (the computer granting logon access)
    - MAC layer address of the FTP client (*hint:* Look in the Ethernet II section of the details pane)
    - MAC layer address of the FTP server
    - Source FTP port number (*hint:* Look in the Transmission Control Protocol section of the details pane)

18. **Click** the **first FTP protocol line item** to select it, **make a screen capture** of the Wireshark window, and **paste** it into the Lab #7 Protocol Analysis document.

> **Note:**
> To capture the screen, **press** the **Ctrl** and **PrtSc** keys together, and then **use Ctrl + V** to paste the image into a Word or other word processor document.

19. **Close** the **Wireshark window.**

> **Note:**
> The next steps will use NetWitness Investigator to examine the same protocol capture file and find specific information needed to complete the deliverables for this lab.

20. **Double-click** the **NetWitness Investigator icon** on the vWorkstation desktop.
21. **Click Collection > New Local Collection** from the NetWitness Investigator toolbar.
22. In the New Local Collection dialog box, **type Lab #7 FTP Analysis** in the Collection Name box and **click OK.**

    When the collection has been created and is ready to use, a new Lab #7 FTP Analysis folder appears in the left Collection pane.
23. **Right-click** the **Lab #7 FTP Analysis collection** and **select Connect** from the context menu.

    When the collection is ready for review, the word *Ready* appears in the Status column.
24. **Right-click** the **Lab #7 FTP Analysis collection** and **select Import Packets** from the context menu.

FIGURE 7.4
Importing packets in NetWitness Investigator

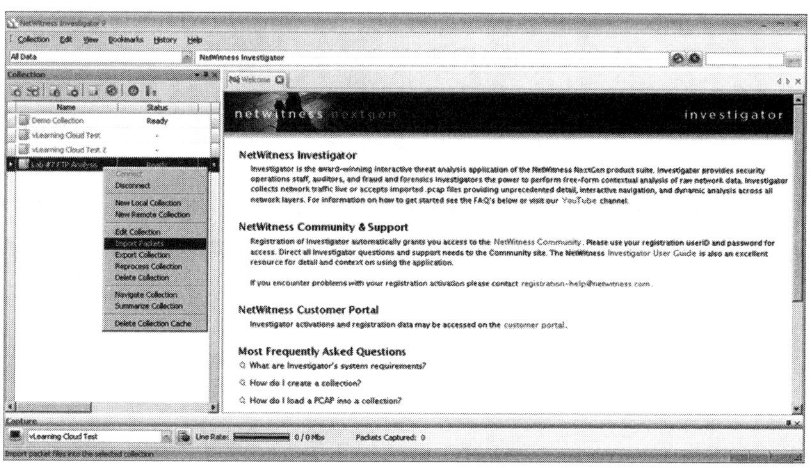

25. In the Open dialog box, **click** the **My Computer icon**.
26. **Double-click** the **Local Drive (C:) icon**.
27. **Double-click** the **Security_Strategies folder**.
28. **Double-click** the **SystemForensics folder**.
29. **Click** the **ftpcapture.pcap file** to select it and **click Open**.

    While importing, the Status column changes to *Importing*. When the packet is ready for analysis, the Status column will change to *Ready*.
30. **Double-click** the **Lab #7 FTP Analysis collection** to open it.

FIGURE 7.5

ftpcapture.pcap in the NetWitness Investigator window

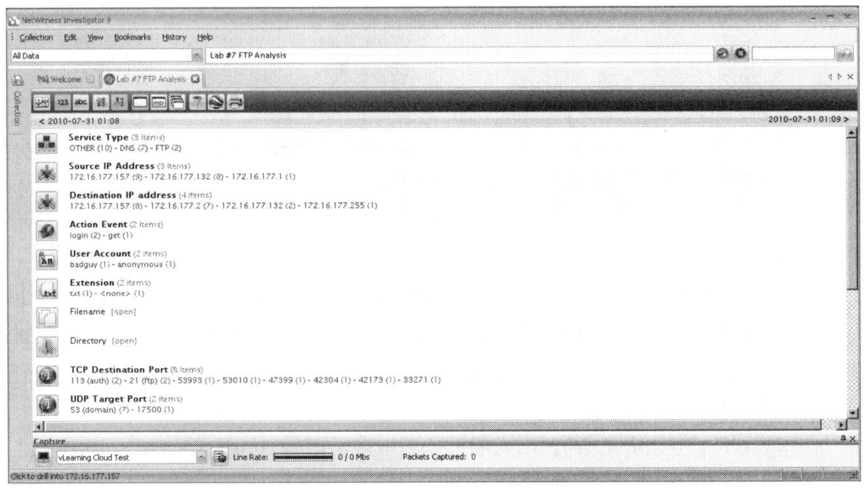

31. **Make a screen capture** of the NetWitness Investigator window showing the ftpcapture.pcap information and **paste** it into the Lab #7 Forensic Analysis document.
32. **Review** the information in NetWitness Investigator, **locate** the following items, and **record** the information in your text document:
    - The names of the two text files that were transferred via FTP
    - The total file size of the FTP file transfer
    - The directory on the FTP server where the two text files are located
    - The user accounts and passwords used to connect to the FTP server
33. **Close** the **NetWitness Investigator window**.
34. **Close** the **OpenOffice.org 3.3 window** and **click Yes** when prompted to save your changes.
35. Use the **File Transfer button** to download the **Lab #7 Protocol Analysis** to your local computer and submit it as part of your deliverables.

Evaluation Criteria and Rubrics

The following are the evaluation criteria and rubrics for Lab #7 that the students must perform:

1. Was the student able to perform forensic protocol analysis on an FTP protocol capture? – [**20%**]
2. Was the student able to examine, at the protocol level, client and server FTP communications using cleartext? – [**20%**]
3. Was the student able to capture and identify logon credentials unencrypted as part of a forensic investigation? – [**20%**]
4. Was the student able to identify FTP client and server TCP/IP communications and dialogue, including three-way handshake and FTP file transfer? – [**20%**]
5. Was the student able to compare Wireshark and NetWitness Investigator as a forensic analysis tool for protocol capture and analysis? – [**20%**]

LAB #7 – ASSESSMENT WORKSHEET

Decode an FTP Protocol Session and Perform Forensic Analysis

Course Name and Number: ______________________________

Student Name: ______________________________

Instructor Name: ______________________________

Lab Due Date: ______________________________

Overview

In this lab, you captured data using Wireshark and explored the forensic capabilities of NetWitness Investigator using the sample protocol capture files provided. You identified cleartext logon communications and IP hosts as well as network devices. You also used NetWitness Investigator to analyze the difference between network cleartext and encrypted communications.

Lab Assessment Questions & Answers

1. Which application and protocol analysis tool helps organize the protocol session and interaction for easier protocol analysis and forensic investigating?

____

____

____

____

2. How are protocol analysis and protocol capturing and archiving linked to digital computer forensic investigations?

____

____

____

____

3. What is the source IP address of the FTP client workstation and FTP server?

4. What is the user account name of the FTP client on the FTP server?

5. What is the MAC layer address of the FTP client workstation and FTP server?

6. What are the names of the two text files that were FTP'd to the server?

7. What was the password in cleartext that was captured?

8. What is the port number for FTP? What would you recommend for securing FTP through the public Internet?

9. What was the total size of the FTP file transfer?

10. What is the directory on the FTP server where the two text files are located?

Automate Image Evaluations and Identify Suspicious or Modified Files

LAB 8

Introduction

Any time forensic investigators explore a machine in search of evidence, they risk changing the very data they seek, potentially invalidating evidence. For this reason, they make use of tools that incorporate write-blocking technologies. The VSCL uses an image of an evidence drive to perform an investigation. In this lab, you will use Paraben's P2 Commander to automate image analysis for highly suspect files that may be useful in a forensic investigation.

Learning Objectives

Upon completing this lab, you will be able to:

- Automate file content examination using Paraben's P2 Commander Highly Suspect listing function during forensic analysis
- Examine in greater detail highly suspect image files
- Sort and analyze image files using P2 Commander's Sorting function
- Identify suspect and highly suspect image files using the Image Analyzer
- Analyze which files are of immediate value for a forensic investigation and include them in a new case file investigation

TOOLS AND SOFTWARE

NAME	MORE INFORMATION
P2 Commander	http://www.paraben.com/p2-commander.html

Deliverables

Upon completion of this lab, you are required to provide the following deliverables to your instructor:

1. A text document containing screen captures of the following:
   a. The number of files in each of P2 Commander's default categories;
   b. The file names and file types for suspect items identified by the Image Analyzer;
2. Lab #8 Digital Forensic Image Analysis Case File.p2c;
3. Lab Assessment Questions & Answers for Lab #8.

Hands-On Steps

1. This lab begins at the student landing vWorkstation virtual machine desktop of the VSCL, as shown here.

FIGURE 8.1

"Student Landing" VSCL workstation

> **Note:**
> The next steps will create a new case file using Paraben's P2 Commander. You will load and sort digital evidence, and identify suspect images using the Image Analyzer.

2. **Double-click** the **OpenOffice.org 3.3 icon** on the desktop to open the application.
3. **Click** the **Text Document icon** to open a new document.
4. At the top of the document, **type *your name and the date and time*** that this file was created.
5. **Click File > Save As** from the toolbar.
6. In the Save As dialog box, **type Lab #8 Digital Forensic Image Analyzer Report** in the File name box.
7. **Select Microsoft® Word 97/2000/XP (.doc)** from the Save as type drop-down menu, **click** the **Desktop icon**, and **click** the **Save button** to save this file to the vWorkstation desktop.

FIGURE 8.2

Saving the OpenOffice document

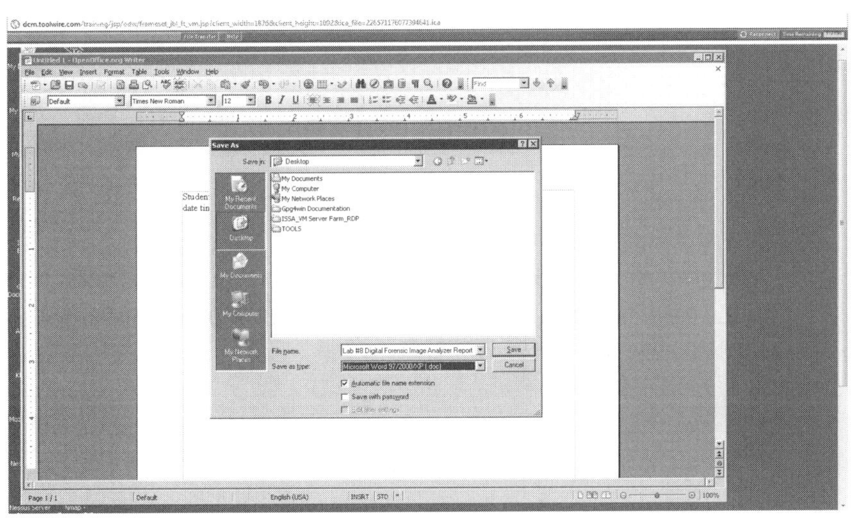

8. **Click** the **Keep Current Format button** if prompted to change the OpenOffice format type.
9. **Double-click** the **P2 Commander JB Learning icon** on the desktop to open the application.

   The P2 Commander's welcome screen opens with a navigation box entitled *Start your work here* at the left containing links to the most common activities that forensic investigators will perform within the tool.
10. **Click** the **Create new case link** in the left navigation box.

FIGURE 8.3

The P2 Commander welcome screen

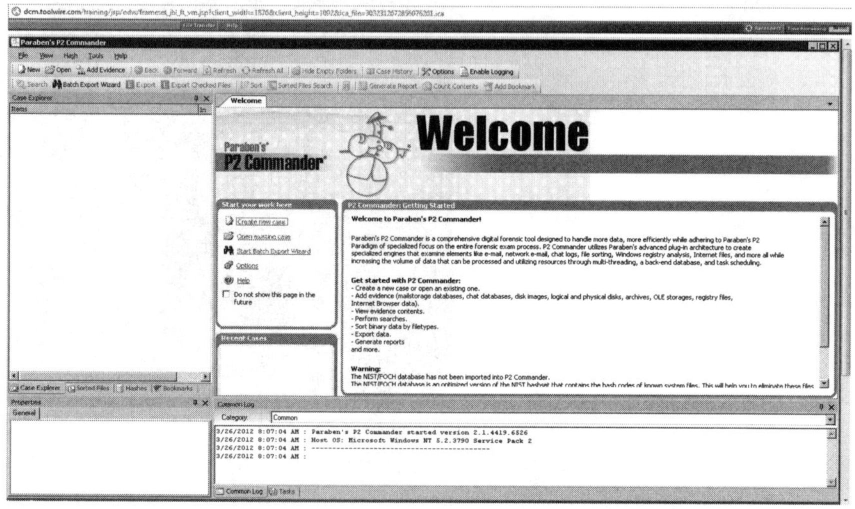

11. In the New Case dialog box, **click** the **Case Properties tab**.
12. **Type Lab #8 Digital Forensic Case File** in the Case name box.

FIGURE 8.4

The New Case dialog box

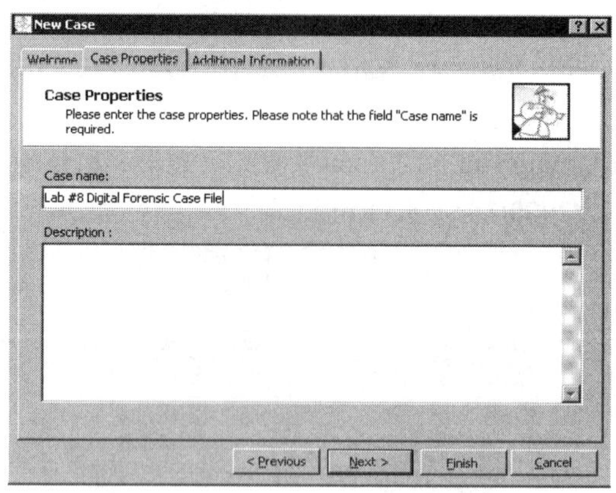

13. **Click** the **Additional Information tab** to continue.
14. **Type *your name*** in the Investigator's name box and **click** the **Finish button**.
15. In the New case creation dialog box, **type Lab #8 Digital Forensic Case File** in the File name box, if necessary.

16. **Click Save** to create the new case file.

    A Lab #8 Digital Forensic Case File tab is added to the P2 Commander screen and the Add New Evidence dialog box opens.

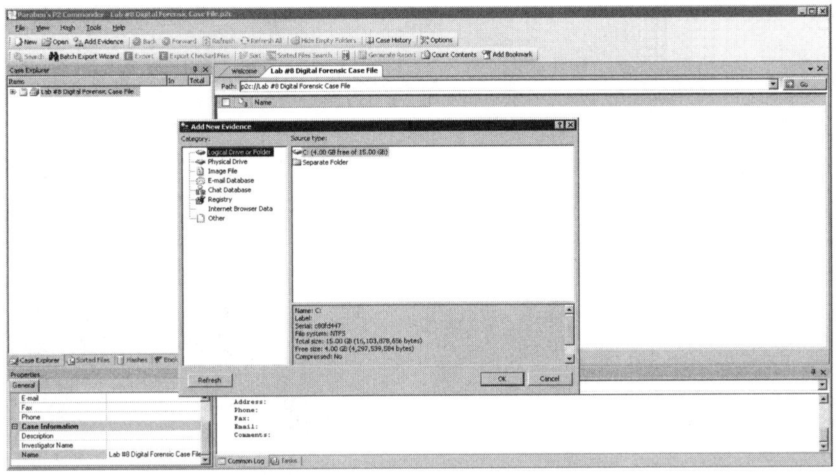

FIGURE 8.5

The Add New Evidence dialog box

17. **Click Image File** in the left pane of the Add New Evidence dialog box.
18. **Click Drive image** in the right pane and **click OK**.

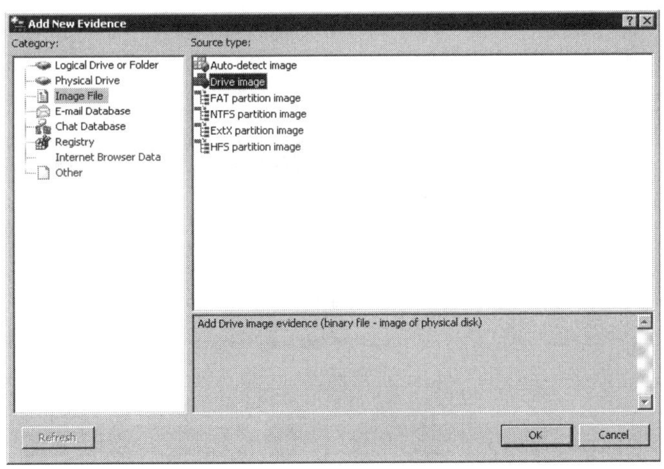

FIGURE 8.6

Adding evidence to the case file

19. In the Open dialog box, **navigate** to the **C:\Forensic_Tools\vm_image folder**, **select** the **evidence_drive.e01.E01 file**, and **click Open**.

20. In the Enter a new evidence name box, **type Lab #8 Forensic Analysis** and **click OK** to add the data from this file to your case file.

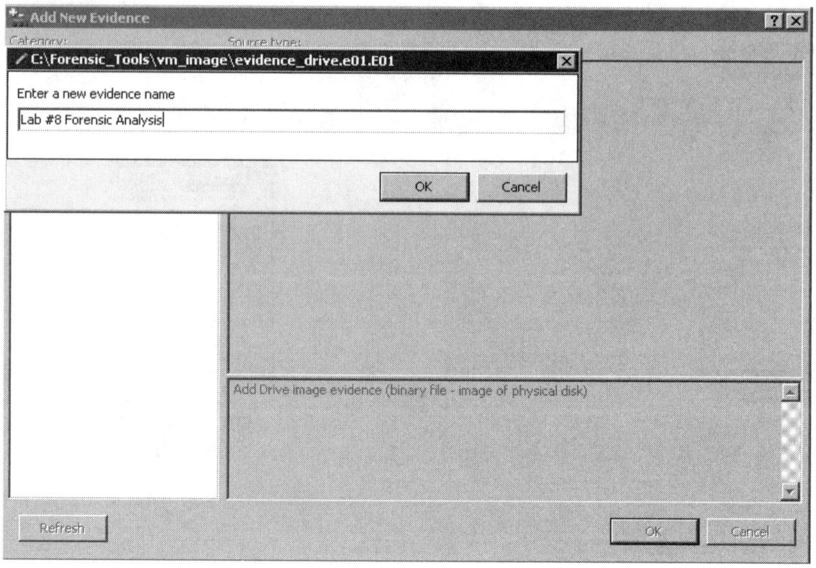

FIGURE 8.7

Identifying the digital image file

21. **Double-click Lab #8 Forensic Analysis** in the right pane of the P2 Commander.
22. **Double-click Partition Parser**.
23. **Double-click Partition0**.

    The NTFS dialog box will pop up.

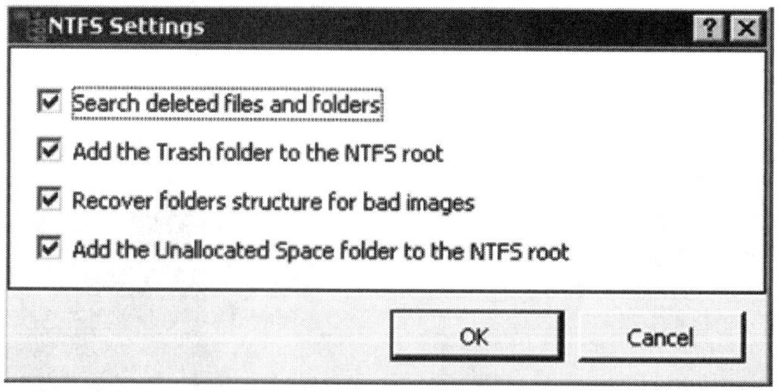

FIGURE 8.8

NTFS Settings dialog box

24. **Verify** that all options in the NTFS Settings dialog box are checked and **click OK**.
25. **Double-click NTFS** in the right pane.
26. **Double-click** the **Root folder** to see the file structure of the evidence image.
27. **Click** the **Lab #8 Digital Forensic Case File folder** in the left Case Explorer pane.
28. **Right-click Lab #8 Forensic Analysis** in the right pane and **select Sorting** from the context menu.

29. **Accept** the **default selections** in the P2 Commander Sorting Engine and **click Finish.**

 This process will take several minutes. When finished, the Completed tab in the bottom pane of the P2 Commander window will show a (1) indicator.

FIGURE 8.9

P2 Commander Sorting Engine

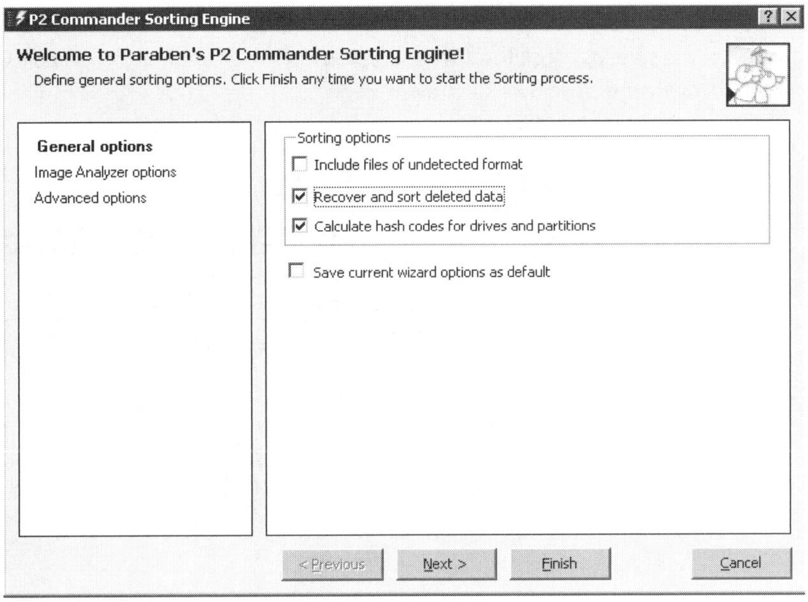

30. **Click** the **Sorted Files tab** in the bottom left pane of the P2 Commander window.

 All of the files that P2 Commander reviewed will appear in the right pane. The Sorted Files tab in this pane displays the total number of files that were sorted. Record the total number of files in the Lab #8 Digital Forensic Image Analyzer Report document.

31. **Double-click** the **Sorted Files item** in the left pane to expand the folder and see the default categories into which P2 Commander sorts the files on the disk image.

 After each category name, P2 Commander indicates the number of files sorted into that category by placing the number within parentheses.

32. With the category list expanded, **make a screen capture** of the P2 Commander window and **paste** it into the Lab #8 Digital Forensic Image Analyzer Report document.

> **Note:**
> To capture the screen, **press** the **Ctrl** and **PrtSc** keys together, and then **use Ctrl + V** to paste the image into a Word or other word processor document.

FIGURE 8.10

P2 Commander sort categories

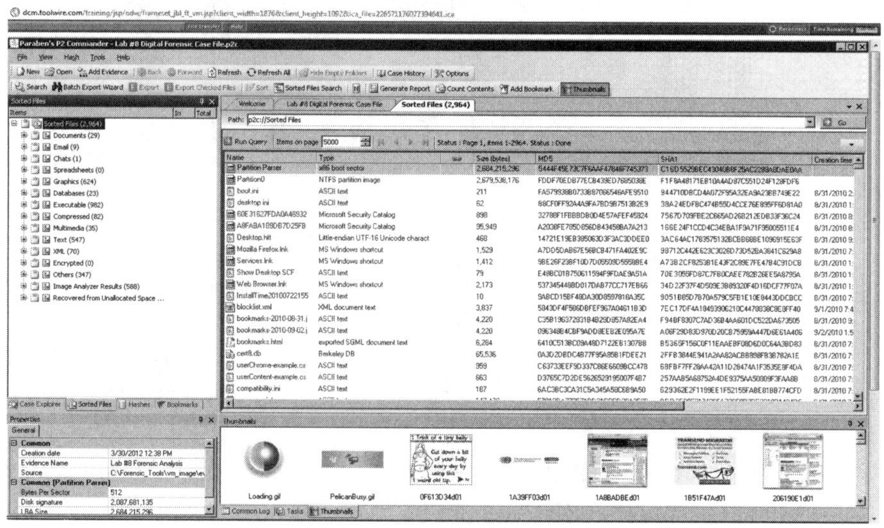

33. **Double-click** the **Image Analyzer Results category** to see the subcategories provided by P2 Commander.
34. In the Lab #8 Digital Forensic Image Analyzer Report document, **document** the number of files in each of the following categories:
    - Low Suspect
    - Suspect
    - Highly Suspect
35. **Click** the **Suspect category** in the left pane of the P2 Commander window to see the list of files identified as *Suspect*.
36. **Make a screen capture** of the P2 Commander window and **paste** it into the Lab #8 Digital Forensic Image Analyzer Report document.
37. **Repeat steps 35-36** for the files in the *Highly Suspect* category.
38. **Close** the **OpenOffice.org 3.3 window** and **click Yes** when prompted to save your changes.
39. **Close** the **P2 Commander window**.
40. Use the **File Transfer button** to download the **text file** to your local computer and submit it as part of your deliverables.

Evaluation Criteria and Rubrics

The following are the evaluation criteria and rubrics for Lab #8 that the students must perform:

1. Was the student able to automate file content examination using Paraben's P2 Commander Highly Suspect listing function during forensic analysis? – [**20%**]
2. Was the student able to examine in greater detail highly suspect image files? – [**20%**]
3. Was the student able to sort and analyze image files using P2 Commander's Sorting function? – [**20%**]
4. Was the student able to identify suspect and highly suspect image files using the Image Analyzer? – [**20%**]
5. Was the student able to analyze which files are of immediate value for a forensic investigation and include them in a new case file investigation? – [**20%**]

LAB #8 – ASSESSMENT WORKSHEET

Automate Image Evaluations and Identify Suspicious or Modified Files

Course Name and Number: ______________________________

Student Name: ______________________________

Instructor Name: ______________________________

Lab Due Date: ______________________________

Overview

Any time forensic investigators explore a machine in search of evidence, they risk changing the very data they seek, potentially invalidating evidence. For this reason, they make use of tools that incorporate write-blocking technologies. The VSCL uses an image of an evidence drive to perform an investigation. In this lab, you used Paraben's P2 Commander to automate image analysis for highly suspect files that may be useful in a forensic investigation.

Lab Assessment Questions & Answers

1. In a child pornography or sex offender case, why would it be important to confiscate and identify the websites and kinds of images found on the accused's laptop or desktop computer?

____

____

____

____

2. Explain what the P2 Commander Image Analyzer does and what it looks for.

____

____

____

____

3. How do you decrease the amount of false positives in the "Highly Suspect" or "Suspect" categories?

4. In how many different categories does P2 Commander's "Sorted Files" list all the identified files? What are these categories?

5. Where would you look to identify if a rogue application, malicious spyware application, or keyboard logger application were loaded on the target evidence_drive?

6. Where would you look to identify ZIP files and compressed files that may actually contain embedded malicious software?

7. Where must you also look to examine possible image files on the evidence_drive under investigation?

8. If you did not have a report-writing "Case History" tool in P2 Commander, what would you have to do to maintain chain of custody while interacting with this evidence_drive?

Craft an Evidentiary Report for a Digital Forensic Case

LAB 9

Introduction

Any time forensic investigators explore a machine in search of evidence, they risk changing the very data they seek, potentially invalidating evidence. For this reason, they make use of tools that incorporate write-blocking technologies. The VSCL uses an image of an evidence drive to perform an investigation. In this lab, you will explore the forensic capabilities of Paraben's P2 Commander by creating an evidentiary report that can be used in a court of law. You will use the sample files found in the lab and eliminate any data that is not pertinent or necessary to the case.

Learning Objectives

Upon completing this lab, you will be able to:

- Adhere to the chain of custody when developing an evidentiary report
- Use Paraben's P2 Commander to generate an evidentiary report that can be submitted in a court of law as actual evidence
- Configure automated reporting to report only the profile and contents of a single suspect or incident
- Create a text report and MD5 hash files generated by P2 Commander as documentation within the evidentiary report
- Craft an executive summary presenting your findings, assessment, and the recommendations of your digital forensic case report

TOOLS AND SOFTWARE

NAME	MORE INFORMATION
P2 Commander	http://www.paraben.com/p2-commander.html

Deliverables

Upon completion of this lab, you are required to provide the following deliverables to your instructor:

1. Lab #9 Digital Forensic Case File.txt;
2. Lab #9 Digital Forensic Case File.txt.MD5;
3. Lab Assessment Questions & Answers for Lab #9.

Hands-On Steps

1. This lab begins at the student landing vWorkstation virtual machine desktop of the VSCL, as shown here.

FIGURE 9.1

"Student Landing" VSCL workstation

> **Note:**
> The next steps will create an evidentiary report for a single user using Paraben's P2 Commander and the sample files provided in this lab.

2. **Double-click** the **P2 Commander JB Learning icon** on the desktop to open the application.

   The P2 Commander's welcome screen opens with a navigation box entitled *Start your work here* at the left containing links to the most common activities that forensic investigators will perform within the tool.
3. **Click** the **Create new case link** in the left navigation box.

FIGURE 9.2

The P2 Commander welcome screen

4. In the New Case dialog box, **click** the **Case Properties tab**.
5. **Type Lab #9 Digital Forensic Case File** in the Case name box.
6. **Click** the **Additional Information tab** to continue.
7. **Type *your name*** in the Investigator's name box and **click** the **Finish button**.
8. In the New case creation dialog box, **type Lab #9 Digital Forensic Case File** in the File name box, if necessary.

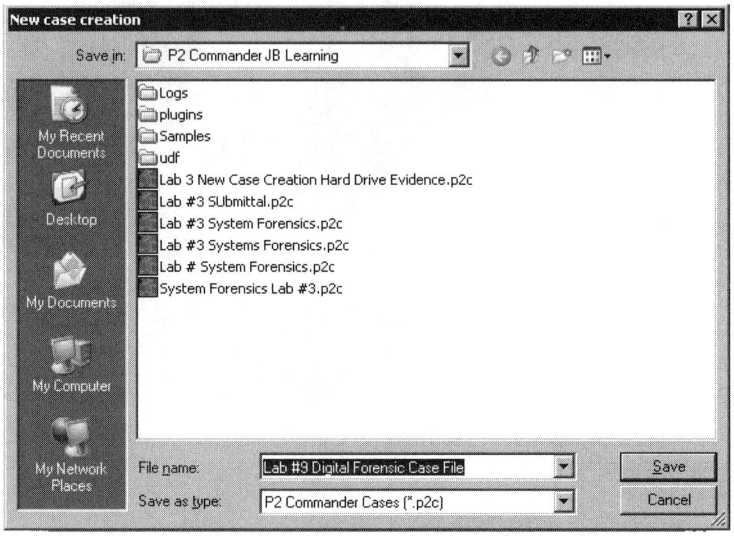

FIGURE 9.3
Creating the new case file

9. **Click Save** to create the new case file.

   A Lab #9 Digital Forensic Case File tab is added to the P2 Commander screen, and the Add New Evidence dialog box opens.
10. **Click Image File** in the left pane of the Add New Evidence dialog box.
11. **Click Drive image** in the right pane and **click OK**.

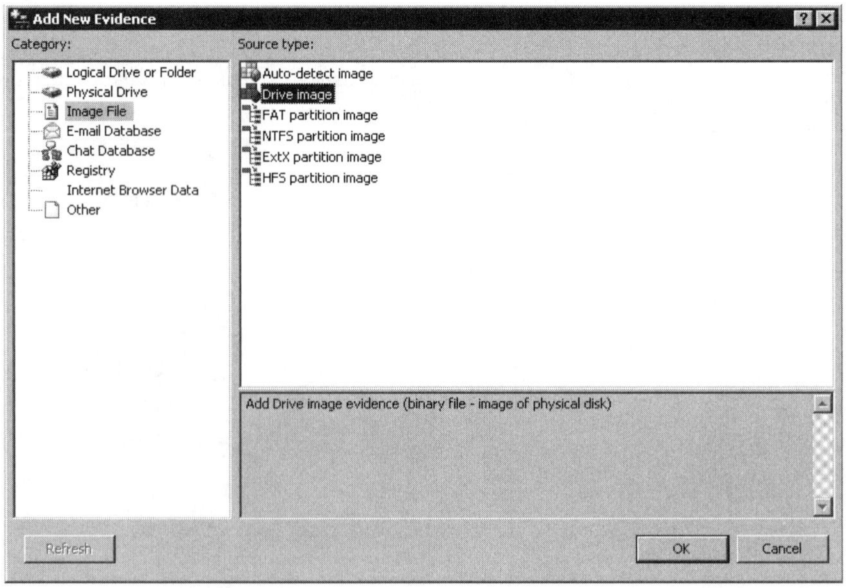

FIGURE 9.4
The Add New Evidence dialog box

12. In the Open dialog box, **navigate** to the **C:\Forensic_Tools\vm_image folder**, **select** the **evidence_drive.e01.E01 file**, and **click Open**.

FIGURE 9.5

Adding evidence to the case file

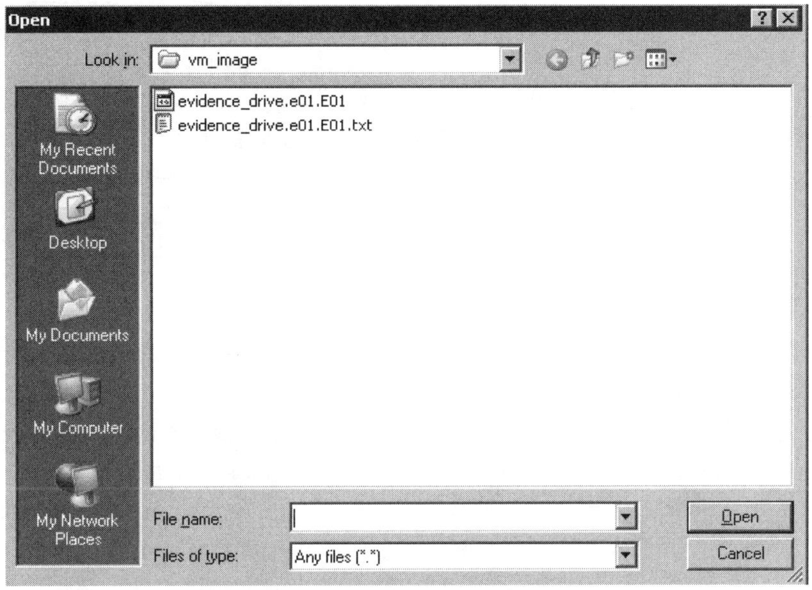

13. In the Enter a new evidence name box, **type Lab #9 Forensic Analysis** and **click OK** to add the data from this file to your case file.

FIGURE 9.6

Identifying the digital image file

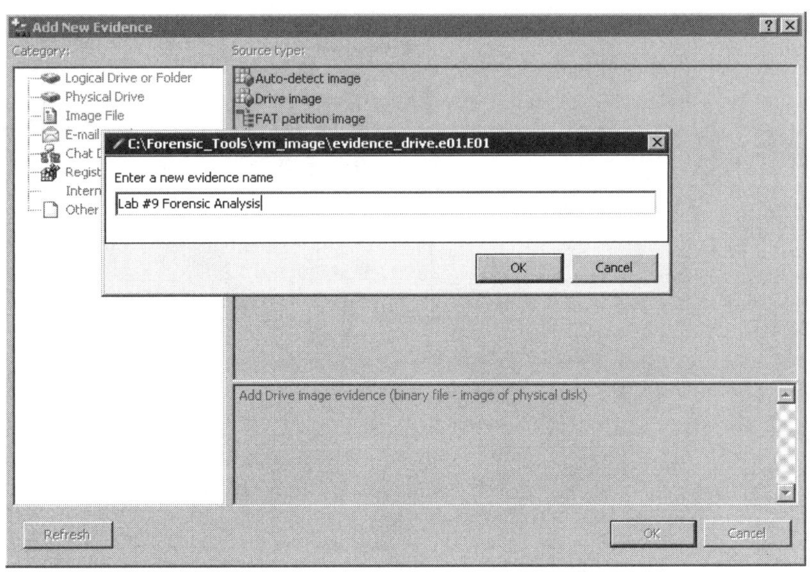

14. **Double-click Lab #9 Forensic Analysis** in the right pane of the P2 Commander.
15. **Double-click Partition Parser**.

16. **Double-click Partition0.**
    The NTFS dialog box will pop up.

FIGURE 9.7
NTFS Settings dialog box

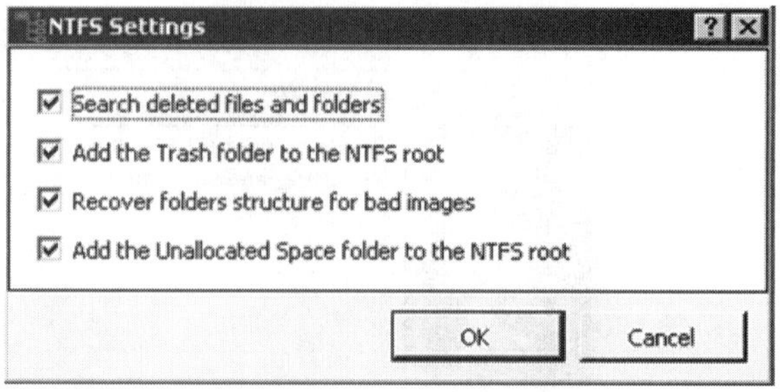

17. **Verify** that all options in the NTFS Settings dialog box are checked and **click OK**.
18. **Double-click NTFS** in the right pane.
19. **Double-click** the **Root folder** to see the file structure of the evidence image.
20. **Click** the **Lab #9 Digital Forensic Case File folder** in the left Case Explorer pane.
21. **Right-click Lab #9 Forensic Analysis** in the right pane and **select Sorting** from the context menu.
22. **Accept** the **default selections** in the P2 Commander Sorting Engine and **click Finish**.
    This process will take several minutes. When finished, the Completed tab in the bottom pane of the P2 Commander window will show a (1) indicator.

FIGURE 9.8
P2 Commander Sorting Engine

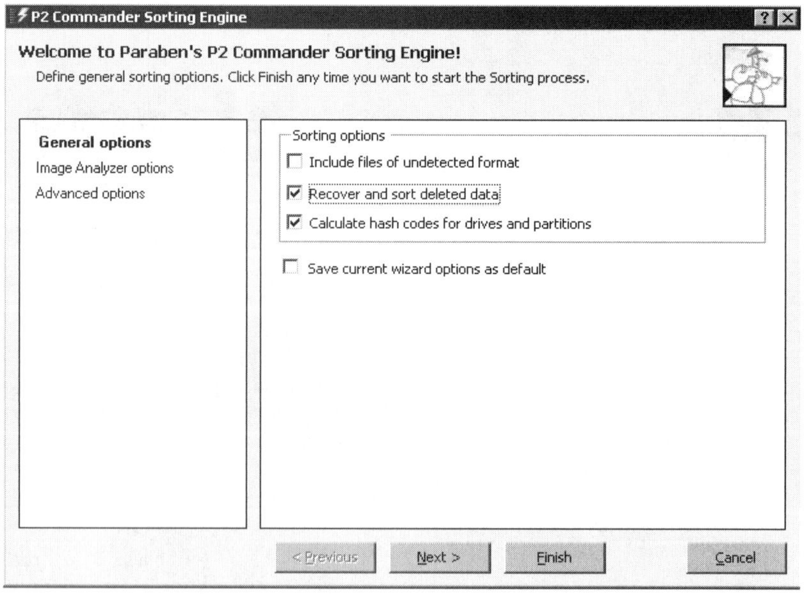

23. **Click** the **Sorted Files tab** in the bottom left pane of the P2 Commander window.
    All of the files that P2 Commander reviewed will appear in the right pane. The Sorted Files tab in this pane displays the total number of files that were sorted.

24. **Double-click** the **Sorted Files item** in the left pane to expand the folder and see the default categories into which P2 Commander sorts the files on the disk image.

    After each category name, P2 Commander indicates the number of files sorted into that category by placing the number within parentheses.

25. **Click** the **Case Explorer tab** in the bottom left pane of the P2 Commander window.
26. **Double-click** the **Lab #9 Digital Forensic Case File item** in the Case Explorer to expand it.

FIGURE 9.9

P2 Commander Case Explorer

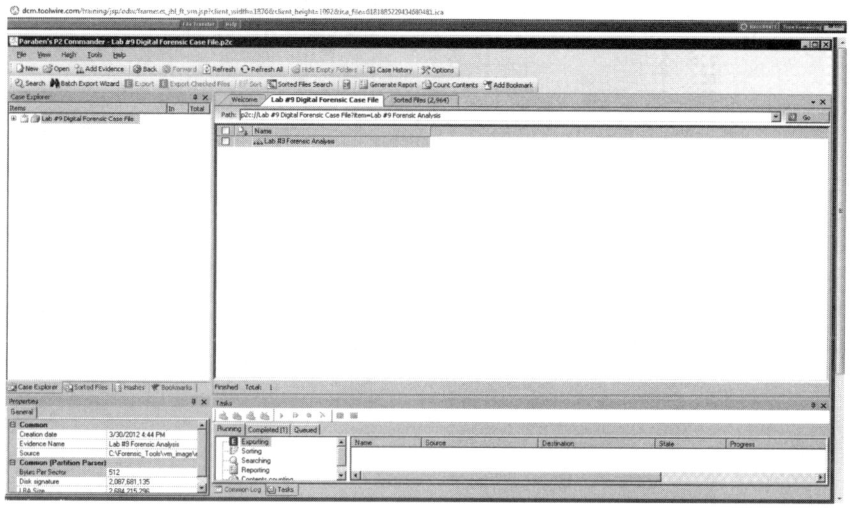

27. **Double-click** the **Partition0 item** in the Case Explorer to expand it.
28. **Double-click** the **NTFS item** in the Case Explorer to expand it.
29. **Double-click** the **Root folder** in the Case Explorer to expand it.
30. **Double-click** the **Documents and Settings folder** in the Case Explorer to expand it.
31. **Click** the **Administrator folder** in the Case Explorer to load the related files into the right pane.
32. In the P2 Commander toolbar, **click File > Generate Report** to open the Reports Wizard.

FIGURE 9.10

Generate a report in P2 Commander

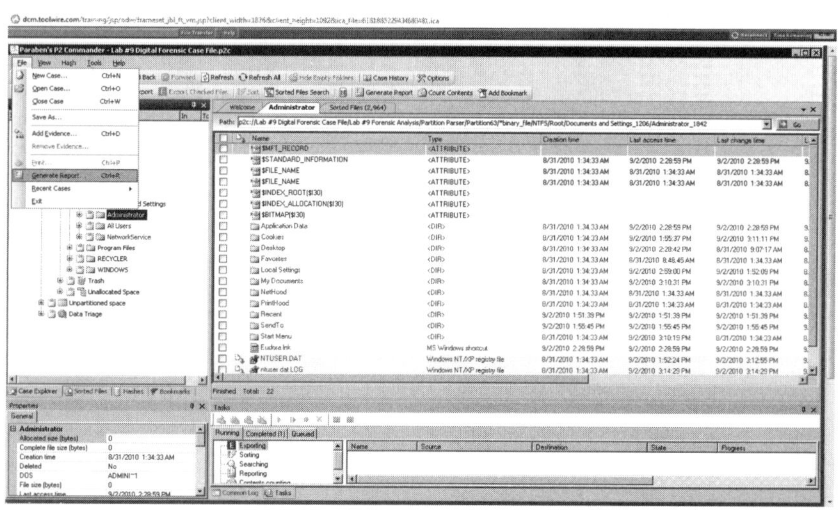

33. **Click** the **Simple Text Report radio button** and **click Next** to continue.

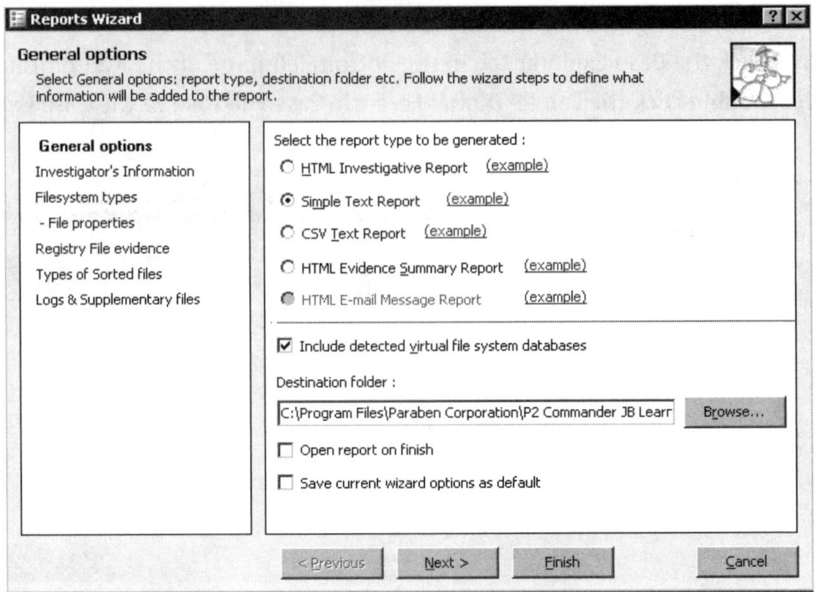

FIGURE 9.11

The Reports Wizard

34. **Type *your name*** in the Investigator's name box and **click Next**.
35. If necessary, **click** the **Include only data checked as "Include to reports" radio button** to specify the file types required for this report.
36. If necessary, **click** the **Add checkbox** to add all file types listed in that column.
37. In the Export column, **click** the **Graphics checkbox** to export only graphic files.
38. **Click** the **Show data by file types (Only for sorted data) radio button** to format the report.

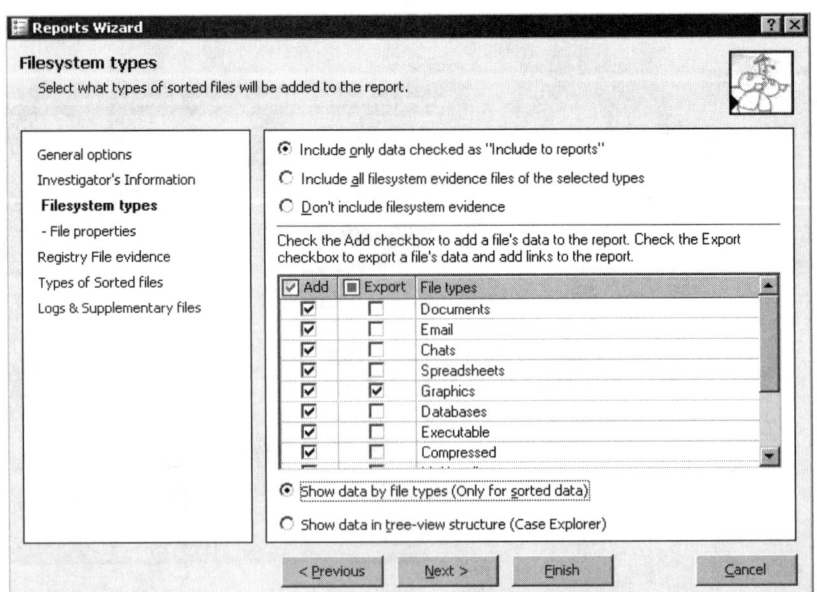

FIGURE 9.12

Selecting filesystem types

39. **Click Next** three times to continue.

40. On the Types of Sorted files page, **click** the **Export checked files checkbox** and **click Next**.

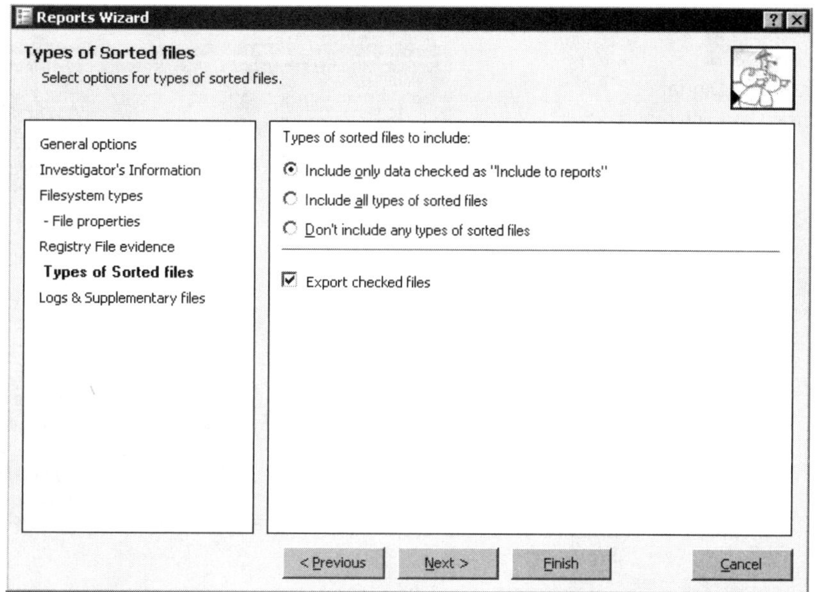

FIGURE 9.13

Selecting the types of sorted files

41. **Click** the **Include Case History checkbox** and **click Finish**.

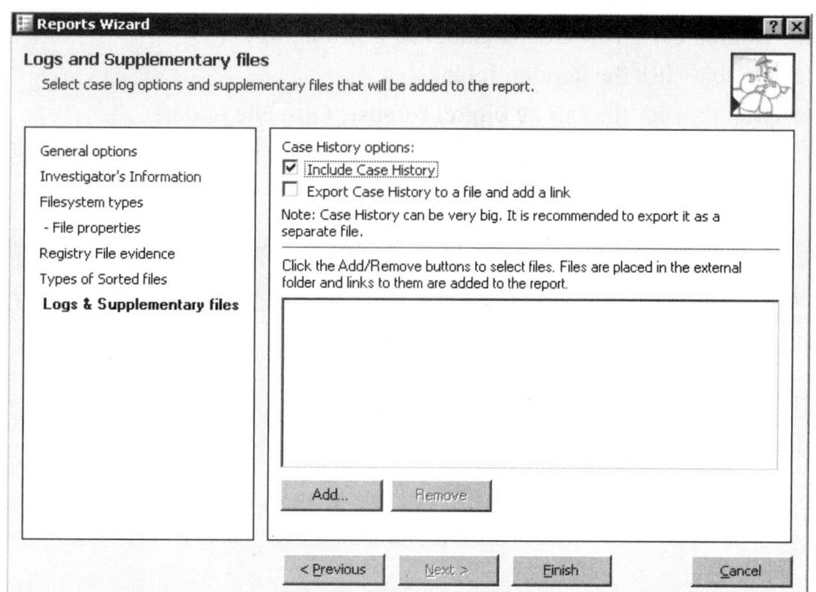

FIGURE 9.14

Selecting logs and supplementary files

42. **Click** the **Completed tab** in the bottom right pane of P2 Commander and click the Reporting (1) icon.

    The completed report is listed as a line item in the bottom right pane. The location of the report file is found in the Destination column.

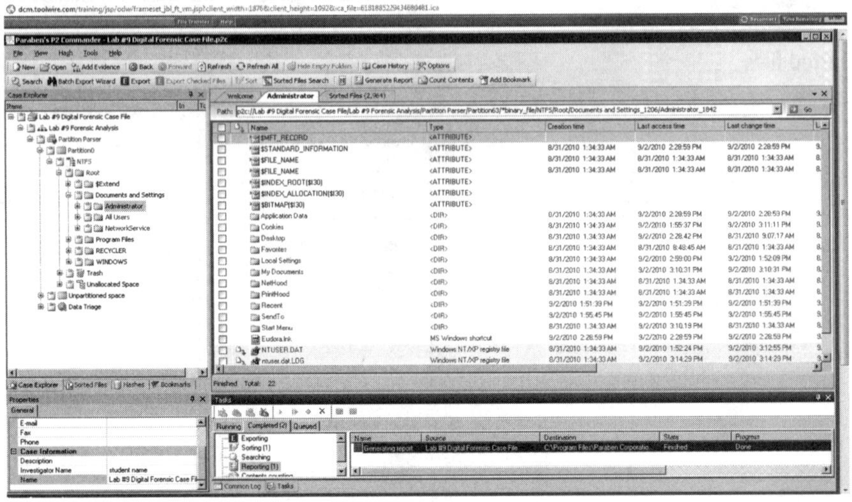

FIGURE 9.15

Locating the Digital Forensic Case File report

43. **Close** the **P2 Commander window**.
44. **Double-click** the **My Computer icon** on the vWorkstation desktop to open the Windows Explorer.
45. **Double-click** the **Local Drive (C:) icon**.
46. **Double-click** the **Program Files folder**.
47. **Double-click** the **Paraben Corporation folder**.
48. **Double-click** the **P2 Commander JB Learning folder**.
49. **Double-click** the **Reports folder**.
50. **Double-click** the **Lab #9 Digital Forensic Case File folder**.

    The folder contains two files: the evidentiary report text file and its MD5 hash file.

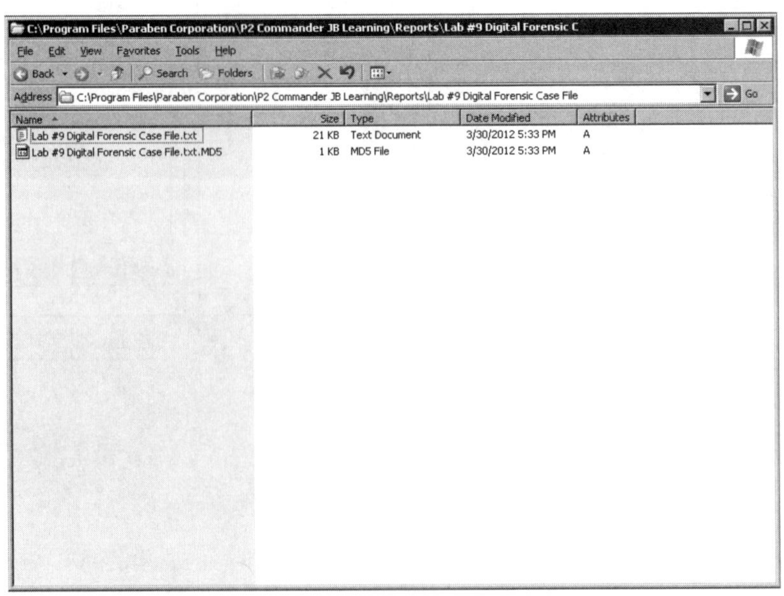

FIGURE 9.16

Navigating to the evidentiary report and its MD5 hash file

51. **Double-click** the **Lab #9 Digital Forensic Case File.txt file** and **review** the contents to understand the format of an evidentiary report.
52. **Close** the **Notepad window.**
53. **Double-click** the **Lab #9 Digital Forensic Case File.txt.MD5 file.**
54. **Click** the **Select the program from a list radio button** on the pop-up window and **click OK.**
55. In the Open With dialog box, **double-click** the **Notepad icon.**

    Windows will associate any future *.MD5 files with the Notepad application. The Lab #9 Digital Forensic Case File.txt.MD5 file will open in the Notepad. Review the contents to understand the format of an MD5 hash file.
56. **Close** the **Notepad window.**
57. **Close** the **Windows Explorer window.**
58. Use the **File Transfer button** to download the **Lab #9 Digital Forensic Case File.txt** report and the **Lab #9 Digital Forensic Case File.txt.MD5 file** to your local computer and submit it as part of your deliverables.

Evaluation Criteria and Rubrics

The following are the evaluation criteria and rubrics for Lab #9 that the students must perform:

1. Was the student able to adhere to the chain of custody when developing an evidentiary report? – **[20%]**
2. Was the student able to use Paraben's P2 Commander to generate an evidentiary report that can be submitted in a court of law as actual evidence? – **[20%]**
3. Was the student able to configure automated reporting to report only the profile and contents of a single suspect or incident? – **[20%]**
4. Was the student able to create a text report and MD5 hash files generated by P2 Commander as documentation within the evidentiary report? – **[20%]**
5. Was the student able to craft an executive summary presenting the findings, assessment, and recommendations of his or her digital forensic case report? – **[20%]**

LAB #9 – ASSESSMENT WORKSHEET

Craft an Evidentiary Report for a Digital Forensic Case

Course Name and Number: ______________________

Student Name: ______________________

Instructor Name: ______________________

Lab Due Date: ______________________

Overview

Any time forensic investigators explore a machine in search of evidence, they risk changing the very data they seek, potentially invalidating evidence. For this reason, they make use of tools that incorporate write-blocking technologies. The VSCL uses an image of an evidence drive to perform an investigation. In this lab, you explored the forensic capabilities of Paraben's P2 Commander by creating an evidentiary report that can be used in a court of law. You used the sample files found in the lab and eliminated any data that was not pertinent or necessary to the case.

Lab Assessment Questions & Answers

1. What is chain of custody?

____

____

____

____

2. Why is chain of custody vital for managing and handling evidence properly?

____

____

____

____

3. What is a write-blocker and why is it necessary to have one in a forensic toolkit?

____

____

____

____

4. When generating and reporting on evidence, why is it important that it be both technically accurate and easy to read?

5. Name three to five items that you should include in computer forensic evidence report.

6. From a computer with direct Internet access, locate three online resources for computer forensic investigative report writing.

7. True/False: It is NOT necessary to document the tools that were used in the forensic investigation.

8. Why is note-taking important during a forensic investigation?

Perform an Incident Response Investigation for a Suspicious Logon

LAB 10

Introduction

Any time forensic investigators explore a machine in search of evidence, they risk changing the very data they seek, potentially invalidating evidence. For this reason, they make use of tools that incorporate write-blocking technologies. The VSCL uses an image of an evidence drive to perform an investigation. In this lab, you will use Paraben's P2 Commander and NetWitness Investigator to identify suspect logon credentials from an FTP packet trace, analyze the digital portion of a forensic image, locate a suspect user file on that image, and create a report to detail your findings.

Learning Objectives

Upon completing this lab, you will be able to:

- Identify suspect logon credentials from an FTP packet trace
- Evaluate information that would be useful to an attacker who has infiltrated the network
- Locate a suspect user profile in a workstation forensic image
- Analyze the digital portion of a forensic investigation and link the two pieces of evidence together to solidify your case
- Create a report detailing findings based on automated reporting of evidence related to a suspect's e-mail communications, identified e-mail attachments, and the protocol capture of the FTP session

TOOLS AND SOFTWARE

NAME	MORE INFORMATION
NetWitness Investigator	http://www.emc.com/security/rsa-netwitness.htm
P2 Commander	http://www.paraben.com/p2-commander.html

Deliverables

Upon completion of this lab, you are required to provide the following deliverables to your instructor:

1. The Lab #10 Digital Forensic Case File.txt evidentiary report;
2. A text document that will serve as an executive summary to the evidentiary report;
3. Lab Assessment Questions & Answers for Lab #10.

Hands-On Steps

1. This lab begins at the student landing vWorkstation virtual machine desktop of the VSCL, as shown here.

FIGURE 10.1
"Student Landing" VSCL workstation

> **Note:**
> The next steps will use NetWitness Investigator to examine a protocol capture file and find specific information needed to complete the deliverables for this lab.

2. **Double-click** the **NetWitness Investigator icon** on the vWorkstation desktop.
3. **Click Collection > New Local Collection** from the NetWitness Investigator toolbar.
4. In the New Local Collection dialog box, **type Lab #10 Forensic Analysis** in the Collection Name box and **click OK**.

   When the collection has been created and is ready to use, a new Lab #10 Forensic Analysis folder appears in the left Collection pane.
5. **Right-click** the **Lab #10 Forensic Analysis collection** and **select Connect** from the context menu.

   When the collection is ready for review, the word *Ready* appears in the Status column.

6. **Right-click** the **Lab #10 Forensic Analysis collection** and **select Import Packets** from the context menu.

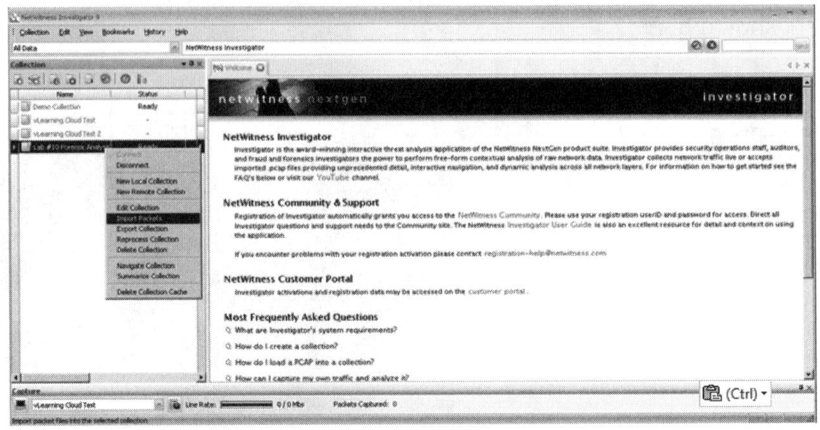

FIGURE 10.2

Importing packets in NetWitness Investigator

7. In the Open dialog box, **click** the **My Computer icon.**
8. **Double-click** the **Local Drive (C:) icon.**
9. **Double-click** the **Security_Strategies folder.**
10. **Double-click** the **SystemForensics folder.**
11. **Click** the **ftpcapture.pcap file** to select it and **click Open.**

    While importing, the Status column changes to *Importing*. When the packet is ready for analysis, the Status column will change to *Ready*.
12. **Double-click** the **Lab #10 Forensic Analysis collection** to open it.
13. In the Service Type section of the window, the FTP service is followed by a (2). This indicates that there were two attempts to open an FTP connection. **Click** that **(2)** to learn more about these attempts.

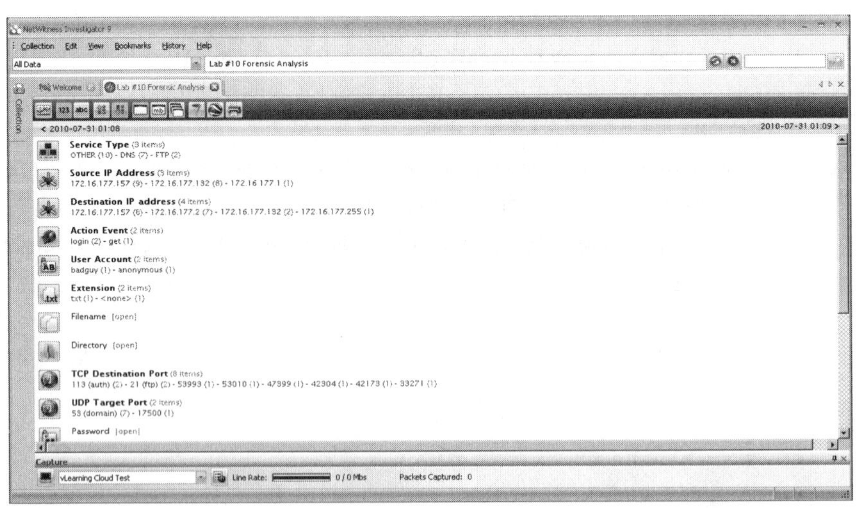

FIGURE 10.3

ftpcapture.pcap in the NetWitness Investigator window

14. **Locate** the following information in NetWitness Investigator; you will need this information to complete the deliverables for this lab:
    - The user accounts and passwords used to connect to the FTP server
    - The names of the two text files that were transferred via FTP
    - The time that the FTP connection was established
    - The IP address of the FTP client and the FTP server

FIGURE 10.4

FTP sessions displayed in NetWitness Investigator

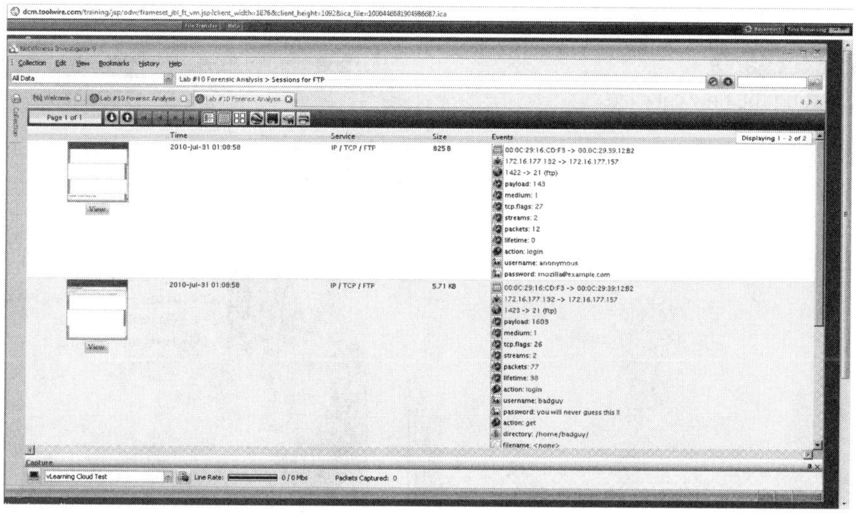

15. **Close** the **NetWitness Investigator window**.

> **Note:**
> The next steps will use Paraben's P2 Commander to perform a forensic image investigation. You will explore the suspect user's e-mail account for evidence.

16. **Double-click** the **P2 Commander JB Learning icon** on the desktop to open the application.

    The P2 Commander's welcome screen opens with a navigation box entitled *Start your work here* at the left containing links to the most common activities that forensic investigators will perform within the tool.

17. **Click** the **Create new case link** in the left navigation box.

FIGURE 10.5

The P2 Commander welcome screen

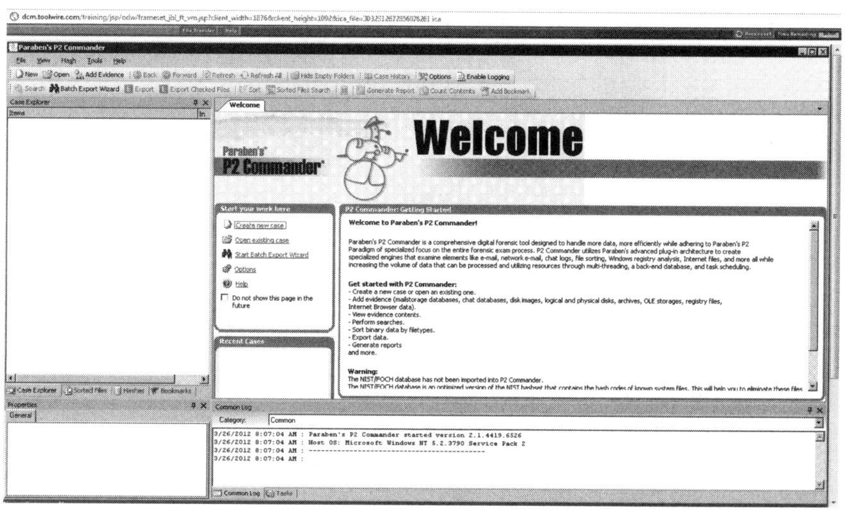

18. In the New Case dialog box, **click** the **Case Properties tab**.
19. **Type Lab #10 Digital Forensic Case File** in the Case name box.
20. **Click** the **Additional Information tab** to continue.
21. **Type *your name*** in the Investigator's name box and **click** the **Finish button**.
22. In the New case creation dialog box, **type Lab #10 Digital Forensic Case File** in the File name box, if necessary.

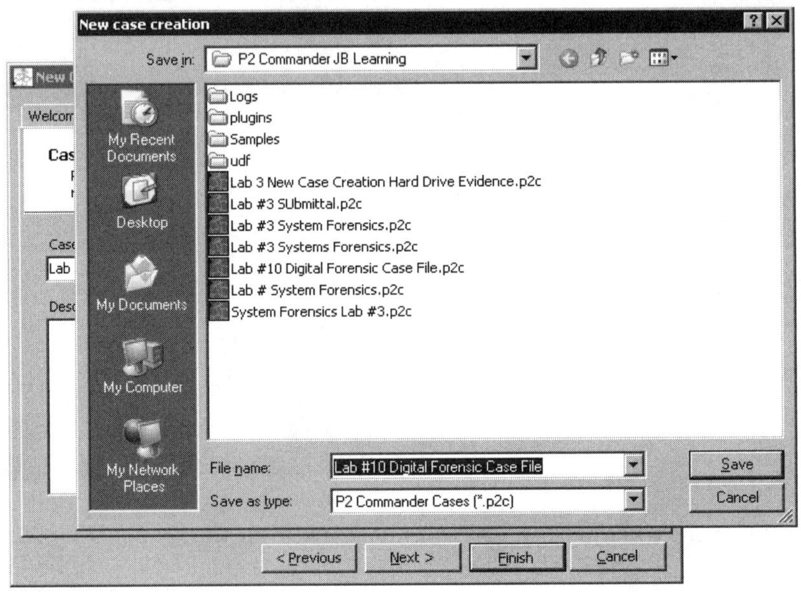

FIGURE 10.6

Creating the new case file

23. **Click Save** to create the new case file.

    A Lab #10 Digital Forensic Case File tab is added to the P2 Commander screen and the Add New Evidence dialog box opens.
24. **Click Image File** in the left pane of the Add New Evidence dialog box.
25. **Click Drive image** in the right pane and **click OK**.

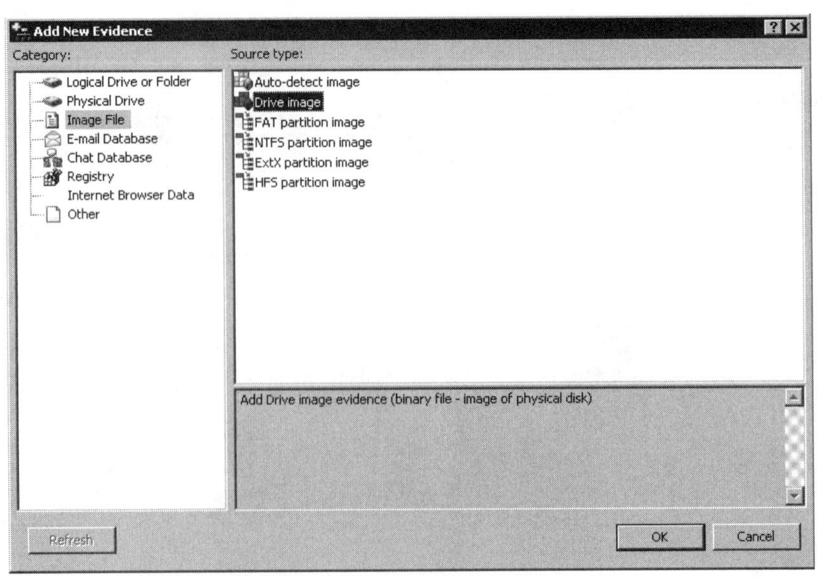

FIGURE 10.7

The Add New Evidence dialog box

26. In the Open dialog box, **navigate** to the **C:\Forensic_Tools\vm_image folder**, **select** the **evidence_drive.e01.E01 file**, and **click Open**.

FIGURE 10.8

Adding evidence to the case file

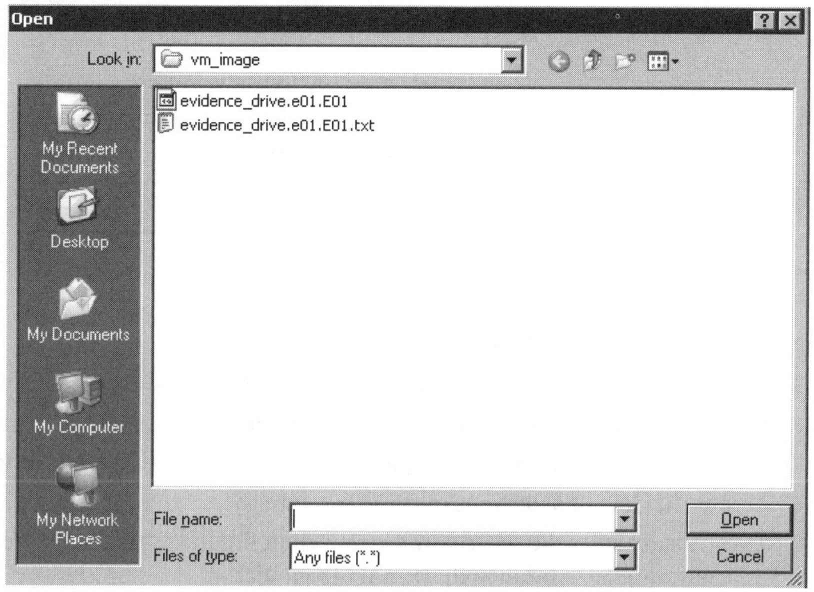

27. In the Enter a new evidence name box, **type Lab #10 Forensic Analysis** and **click OK** to add the data from this file to your case file.

FIGURE 10.9

Identifying the digital image file

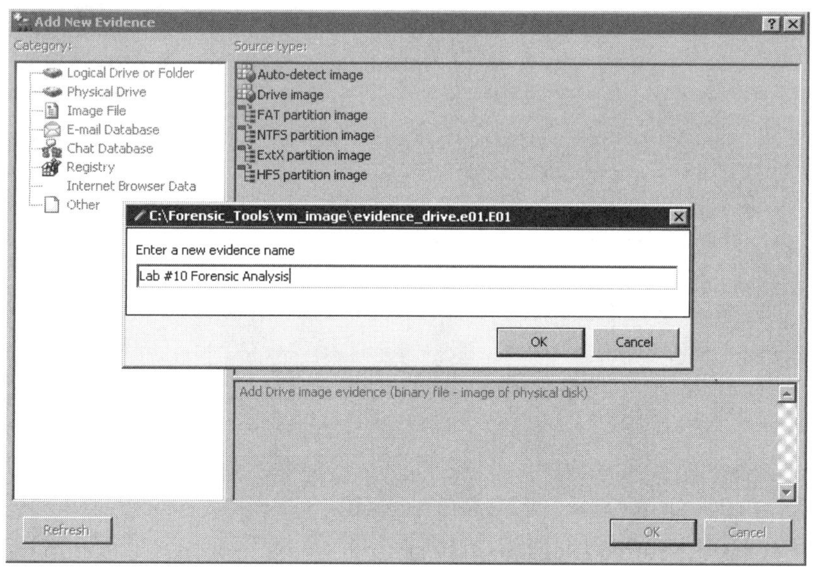

28. **Double-click Lab #10 Forensic Analysis** in the right pane of the P2 Commander.
29. **Double-click Partition Parser**.
30. **Double-click Partition0**.

    The NTFS dialog box will pop up.

31. **Verify** that all options in the NTFS Settings dialog box are checked and **click OK**.

FIGURE 10.10

NTFS Settings dialog box

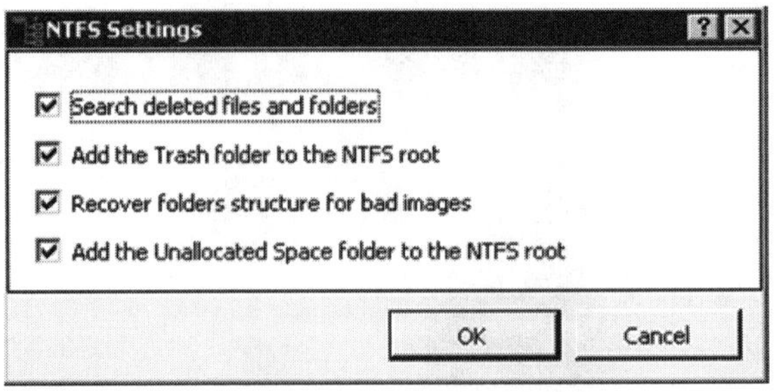

32. **Double-click NTFS** in the right pane.
33. **Double-click** the **Root folder** to see the file structure of the evidence image.
34. **Click** the **Lab #10 Digital Forensic Case File folder** in the left Case Explorer pane.
35. **Right-click Lab #10 Forensic Analysis** in the right pane and **select Sorting** from the context menu.
36. **Accept** the **default selections** in the P2 Commander Sorting Engine and **click Finish**.

    This process will take several minutes. When finished, the Completed tab in the bottom pane of the P2 Commander window will show a (1) indicator.

FIGURE 10.11

P2 Commander Sorting Engine

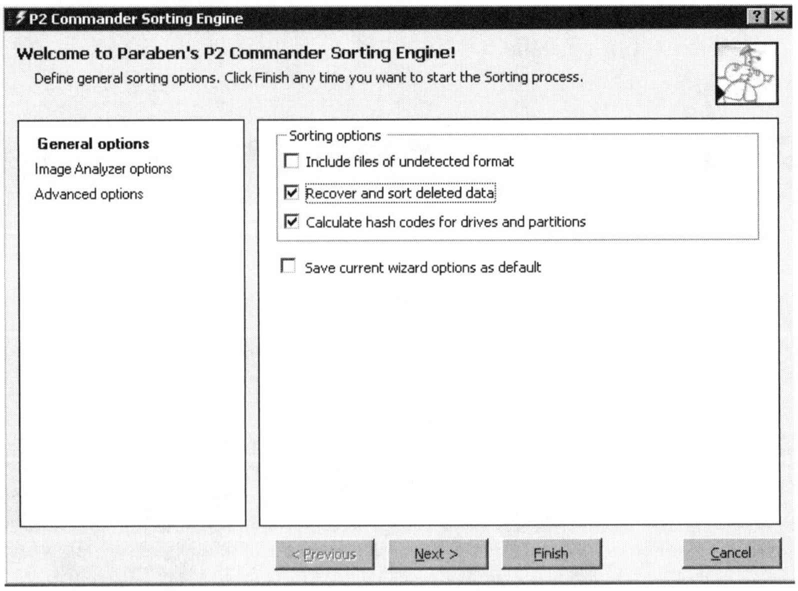

37. **Click** the **Sorted Files tab** in the bottom left pane of the P2 Commander window.

    All of the files that P2 Commander reviewed will appear in the right pane. The Sorted Files tab in this pane displays the total number of files that were sorted.

38. **Double-click** the **Sorted Files item** in the left pane to expand the folder and see the default categories into which P2 Commander sorts the files on the disk image.

    After each category name, P2 Commander indicates the number of files sorted into that category by placing the number within parentheses.

39. **Click E-mail** to load information about the Eudora e-mail usage on this machine.
40. In the right pane, **double-click Out.mbx** to start the process of reading the e-mail file.
41. **Click No** when prompted to mount the Folder Eudora as a database.

    When the process is completed, the right pane of the P2 Commander will list the outgoing e-mail messages that have been stored in this machine.

FIGURE 10.12
Eudora database prompt

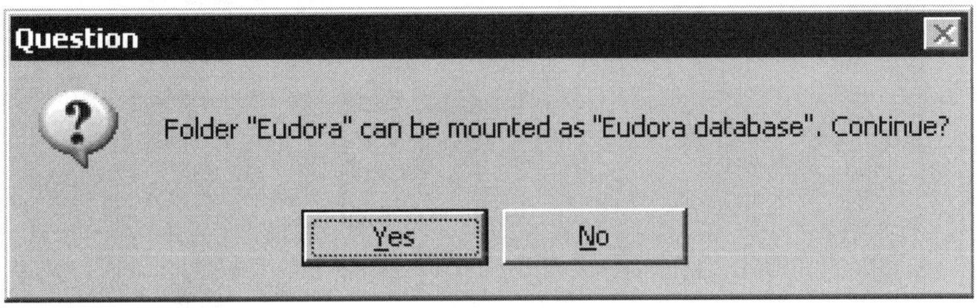

42. **Double-click** the **Out.mbx folder** in the details pane.
43. **Double-click** the **$DATA folder** in the details pane.
44. **Double-click** the **Eudora mailbox** in the details pane.

    There are three messages in the Eudora outbox.

FIGURE 10.13
Eudora outbox in the P2 Commander

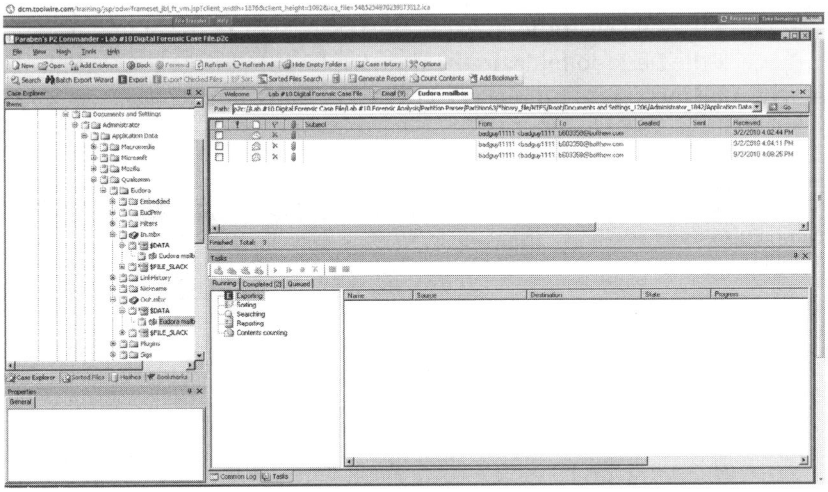

45. **Click** the **first e-mail** in the list and **click** the **E-mail Data tab** at the bottom right of the P2 Commander window.

    The E-mail Data window includes three buttons at the bottom of the window: RFC Header, Text, and Attachments. Click each of these buttons to read the entire message.

FIGURE 10.14

E-mail Data window in P2 Commander

46. **Locate** the following information; you will need this information to complete the deliverables for this lab:
    - The recipient address for these messages
    - The location of the attached text messages
47. **Double-click** the **E-mail Data window** to close it.
48. **Repeat steps 45-47** with each of the messages in the outbox.
49. **Click** the **Administrator folder** in the Case Explorer to expand it.
50. **Click** the **Desktop folder** in the Case Explorer to locate the text files that were attached in the e-mail messages you reviewed in steps 45-46.

FIGURE 10.15

Exploring the Administrator's desktop

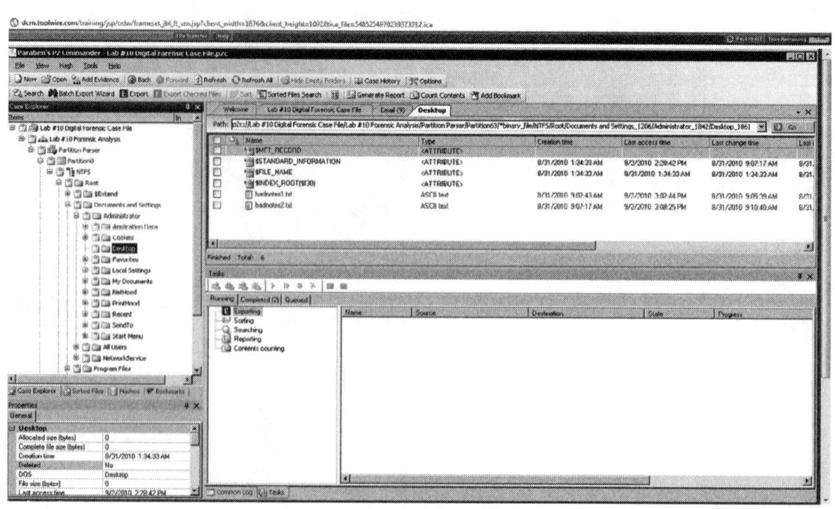

51. **Click** the **badnotes1.txt** and review the content of this file in the bottom right pane.
52. **Click** the **badnotes2.txt** and review the content of this file in the bottom right pane.

> **Note:**
> The next steps will use Paraben's P2 Commander to generate an evidentiary report of the suspect's e-mail account.

53. **Double-click** the **Application Data folder** in the Case Explorer to expand it.
54. **Double-click** the **Qualcomm folder** in the Case Explorer to expand it.
55. **Right-click** the **Eudora folder** to select the e-mail files.
56. In the P2 Commander toolbar, **click File > Generate Report** to open the Reports Wizard.

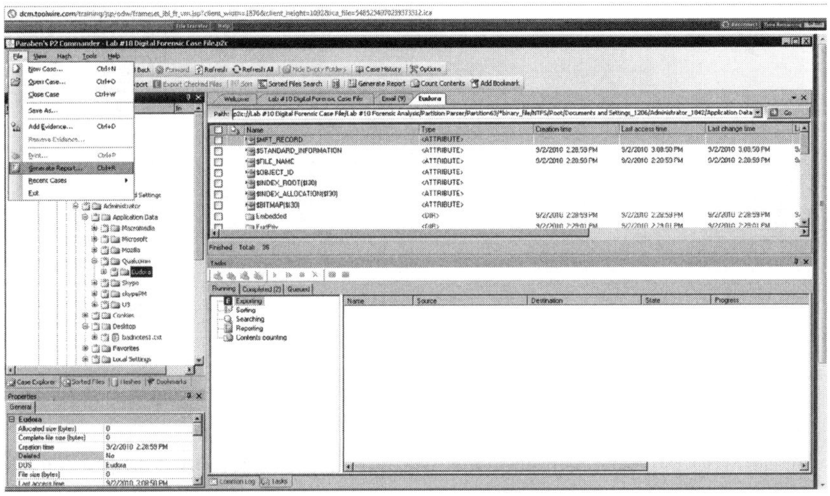

FIGURE 10.16
Generate a report in P2 Commander

57. **Click** the **Simple Text Report radio button** and **click Next** to continue.

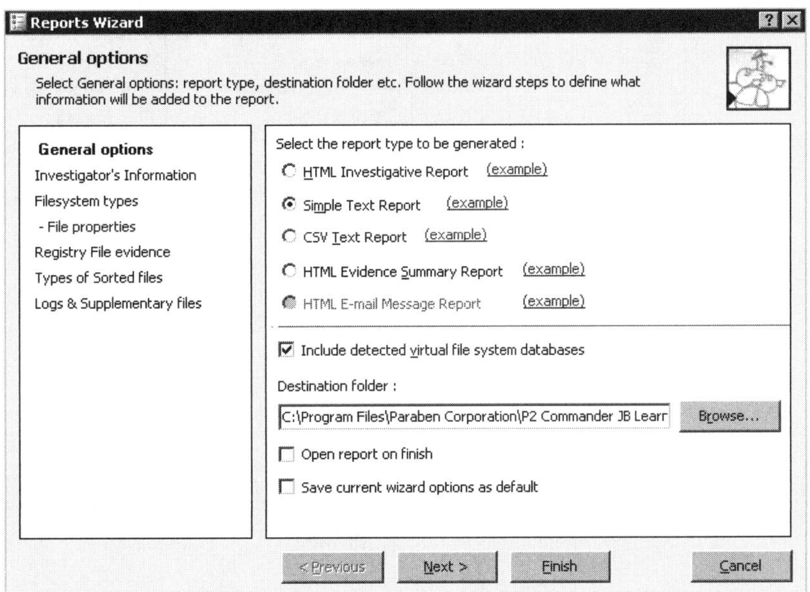

FIGURE 10.17
The Reports Wizard

58. **Type *your name*** in the Investigator's name box and **click Next.**
59. If necessary, **click** the **Include only data checked as "Include to reports" radio button** to specify the file types required for this report.
60. **Click** the **Chats checkbox** in the Add column to exclude chats from the report.
61. **Click** the **Show data by file types (Only for sorted data) radio button** to format the report.

FIGURE 10.18

Selecting filesystem types

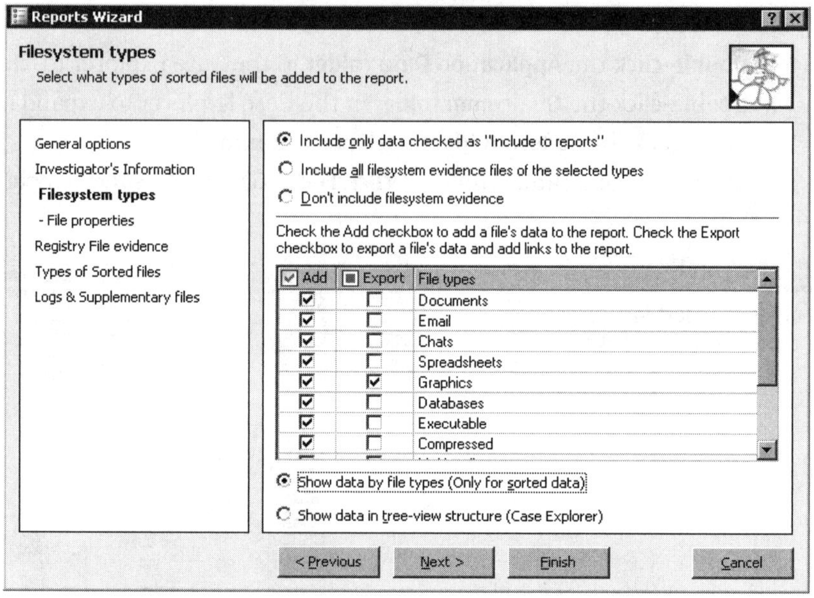

62. **Click Next** three times to continue.
63. On the Types of Sorted files page, **click** the **Export checked files checkbox** and **click Next.**

FIGURE 10.19

Selecting the types of sorted files

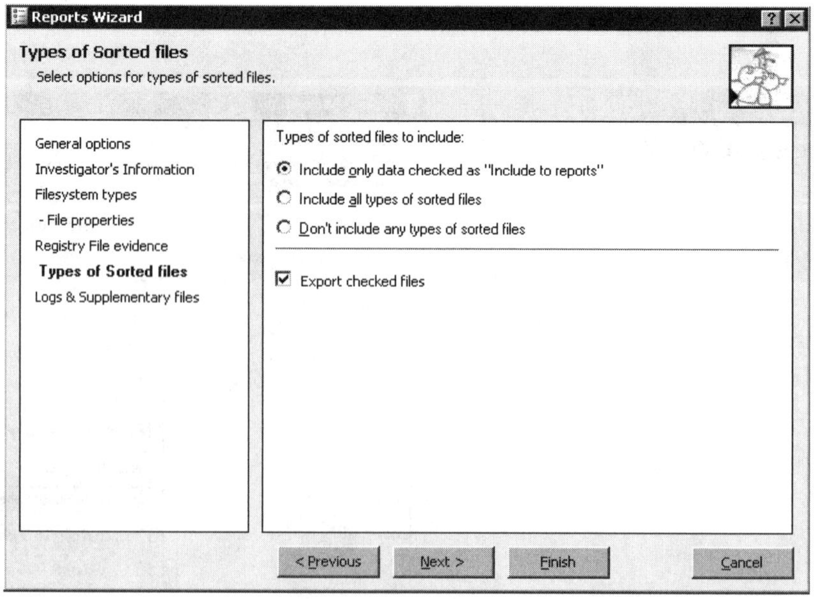

64. **Click** the **Include Case History checkbox** and **click Finish**.

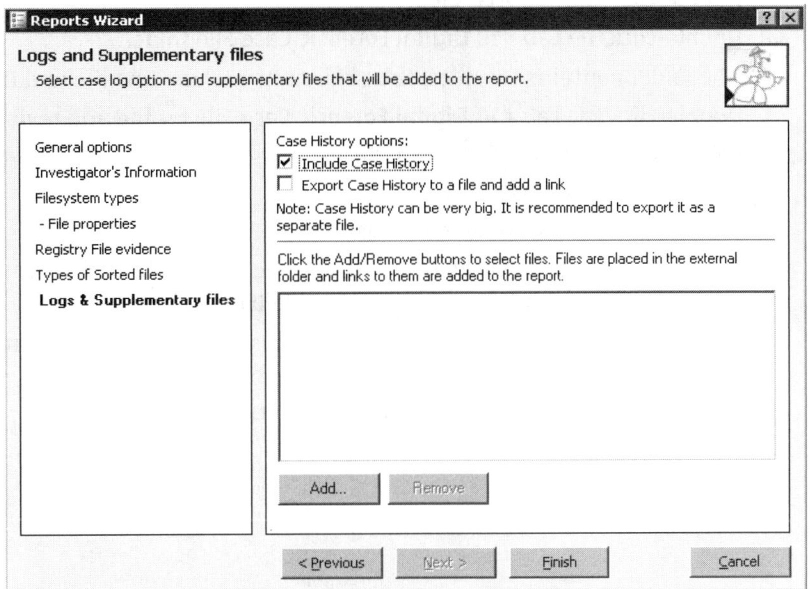

FIGURE 10.20
Selecting logs and supplementary files

65. **Click** the **Completed tab** in the bottom right pane of P2 Commander and click the Reporting (1) icon. The completed report is listed as a line item in the bottom right pane. The location of the report file is found in the Destination column.

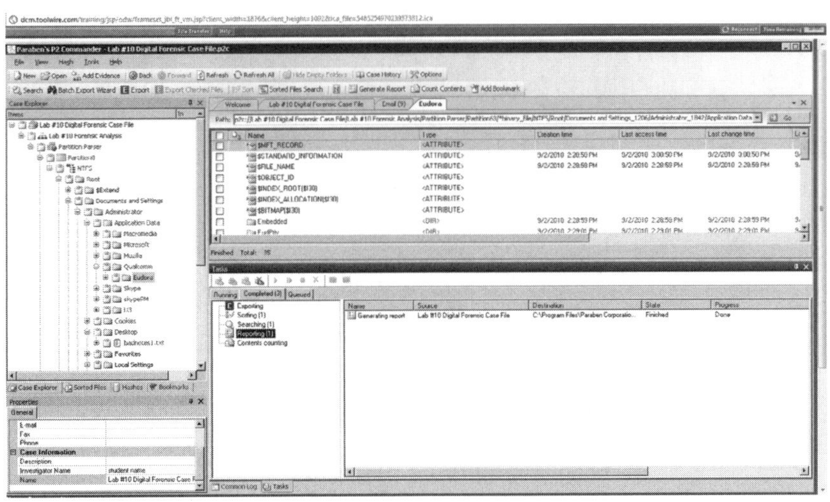

FIGURE 10.21
Locating the Digital Forensic Case File report

66. **Close** the **P2 Commander window**.
67. **Double-click** the **My Computer icon** on the vWorkstation desktop to open the Windows Explorer.
68. **Double-click** the **Local Drive (C:) icon**.
69. **Double-click** the **Program Files folder**.

70. **Double-click** the **Paraben Corporation folder**.
71. **Double-click** the **P2 Commander JB Learning folder**.
72. **Double-click** the **Reports folder**.
73. **Double-click** the **Lab #10 Digital Forensic Case File folder**.
    The folder contains two files: the evidentiary report text file and its MD5 hash file.
74. **Double-click** the **Lab #10 Digital Forensic Case File.txt file** and **review** the contents to understand the format and contents of the evidentiary report.
75. **Close** the **Notepad window**.
76. **Close** the **Windows Explorer window**.
77. Use the **File Transfer button** to download the **Lab #10 Digital Forensic Case File.txt** report to your local computer and submit it as part of your deliverables.
78. Using the information you have used in this and previous labs, **create an executive summary** for this report explaining the tasks, steps, evidence, and facts uncovered that conform to the chain of custody rules. **Submit** this file as part of your deliverables.

Evaluation Criteria and Rubrics

The following are the evaluation criteria and rubrics for Lab #10 that the students must perform:

1. Was the student able to identify suspect logon credentials from an FTP packet trace? – [**20%**]
2. Was the student able to evaluate information that would be useful to an attacker who has infiltrated the network? – [**20%**]
3. Was the student able to locate a suspect user profile in a workstation forensic image? – [**20%**]
4. Was the student able to analyze the digital portion of a forensic investigation and link the two pieces of evidence together to solidify the case? – [**20%**]
5. Was the student able to create a report detailing findings based on automated reporting of evidence related to a suspect's e-mail communications, identified e-mail attachments, and the protocol capture of the FTP session? – [**20%**]

LAB #10 – ASSESSMENT WORKSHEET

Perform an Incident Response Investigation for a Suspicious Logon

Course Name and Number: ______________________

Student Name: ______________________

Instructor Name: ______________________

Lab Due Date: ______________________

Overview

Any time forensic investigators explore a machine in search of evidence, they risk changing the very data they seek, potentially invalidating evidence. For this reason, they make use of tools that incorporate write-blocking technologies. The VSCL uses an image of an evidence drive to perform an investigation. In this lab, you used Paraben's P2 Commander and NetWitness Investigator to identify suspect logon credentials from an FTP packet trace, analyze the digital portion of a forensic image, locate a suspect user file on that image, and create a report to detail your findings.

Lab Assessment Questions & Answers

1. What was the user account name of the FTP client on the FTP server, and which was its IP address?

____

____

____

____

2. How many e-mails did the alleged offender send to his partner before downloading the implicated file? Which are the two e-mail addresses involved?

____

____

____

____

3. As a forensic investigator, would you be able to play back an entire TCP session if it is requested under trial?

____

____

____

____

4. What time did the alleged offender choose to perform the actions? Why do you think this is particularly important? Where did you get this information from?

____

____

____

____

5. What is the name of the "local user" account involved in the alleged actions? Which was the IP address of the alleged offender workstation?

____

____

____

____

6. How many attempts to access the FTP server did you find during the packet capture analysis? Why is this important for your case?

____

____

____

____

7. What was the password of the FTP client account used to perform the alleged actions? How were you able to obtain the password?

____

____

____

____

8. In the absence of a report writing tool like the one within Paraben's P2 commander, how would you keep a proper chain of custody for all of this information as a computer forensic investigator?

___

___

___

___